Best Walks
IN THE CAPE PENINSULA

MIKE LUNDY'S
BEST WALKS
IN THE CAPE PENINSULA

STRUIK

ACKNOWLEDGEMENTS

First and foremost my thanks go to Jose Burman: although we have never met, he is responsible, through his wonderfully descriptive books on hiking in the Western Cape, for getting me onto the mountain in the first place.
A book of this nature is not written without considerable help, and I would like to thank all those who so willingly assisted me in this task:
Marilyn Harcourt-Wood for typing the text and constantly correcting my spelling.
John Robertson and Paul Pigneguy, my regular companions on most of these walks.
Derick Louw of The Movie Studio, for his information on the Lion's Head Gold Mining Syndicate.
Ann Walton for her illustrations.
Amanda de Jongh of the Department of Surveys and Mapping in Mowbray for her cheerful helpfulness, and Zane Erasmus, Forester at Cecilia Forest Station.
To experts in their various fields for their perceptive comments, in particular Ernst Baard and Atherton de Villiers, herpetologists at the Department of Nature and Environmental Conservation, Jonkershoek; Dr Bill Borchers, retired geologist, and Dr Roger Smith, palaentologist at the South African Museum; and Peter Steyn, well-known ornithologist.

Maps: Details from the maps have been reproduced under the Government Printer's Copyright Authority 9115 of 22nd August 1990.

Struik Publishers (Pty) Ltd
(a member of The Struik Group (Pty) Ltd)
Struik House
Oswald Pirow Street
Foreshore
Cape Town 8001

Reg No.: 60/00203/07

First published 1991

Copyright text © Mike Lundy 1991
Cover photographs © Mike Lundy 1991
Copyright maps © Euan Waugh 1991

ISBN 1 86825 175 6

Editor: Jan Schaafsma
Illustrator: Ann Walton
DTP conversion by Bellset, Cape Town
Reproduction of cover by Fotoplate (Pty) Ltd,
Cape Town
Printed and bound by Mills Litho (Pty) Ltd,
Cape Town

CONTENTS

Dedicated to my family:
Eileen, Anton, Guy and Timothy

'When we reach the mountain summits, we leave behind us all the things that weigh heavily on our body and spirit. We leave behind all sense of weakness and depression. We feel a new freedom, a great exhilaration, and exaltation of the body no less than of the spirit.'

Jan Christiaan Smuts

FOREWORD

Among the many contrasts and nuances of beauty and mood that make up South Africa, those of the Cape Peninsula, with its marvellous combination of sea, sky and mountain, are outstanding. This is the environment that Mike Lundy has chosen to write about, presenting the reader with a choice of carefully selected walks, many of which traverse the slopes and heights of Table Mountain. Giving practical advice on such vital aspects as mountain safety and capricious local weather conditions, he skilfully guides his reader through an area that lies within one of the six great floral kingdoms of the world. Table Mountain alone, supporting more than 1 400 flowering plant species, is unparalleled in the enormous variety that occurs within so small a compass.

The potential reward for those seeking environmental and recreational inspiration is enormous. May they, like the author, hold fast to the idea that the pleasure we derive from our natural heritage must not blind us to our responsibility to conserve that heritage for future generations; may they also come to recognise that the environment is a pearl of great price. To protect this pearl mere talk of ecosystems, species and habitats is not enough. Instead we must live in awe of the senses, of light and shade and changing seasons, of life in an unspoilt environment. The author makes us aware of all these aspects. To those who tramp but do not trample underfoot, his message is an open invitation, not merely to visit but to climb and become involved.

I've had the privilege of exploring this great mountain system over a lifetime and the experience has been unbelievably enriching and a constant source of joy and inspiration to me.

The Table, a symbol of hospitality, invites you. Mike Lundy has prepared a fantastic menu of walks. A great feast awaits you.

KENT DURR
MINISTER OF TRADE AND INDUSTRY
AND TOURISM

INTRODUCTION

Who can really say which are the best walks in the Cape Peninsula? When so many variables come into play, it is impossible to be objective, but I do believe that most of the ones I have chosen will appeal to most hikers most of the time.

The walks are extremely varied, as is Mother Mountain herself, and range from an easy walk along the beach to some real cliffhangers, though ropes are not required on any of the walks or climbs. There is something, I believe, to suit all tastes.

I have continued with the simple but descriptive grading system successfully introduced in *Twenty Walks Around Hout Bay*. When taken into account along with the duration of the walk, it should give you a fairly accurate picture of what to expect. The grading system makes allowance for people who suffer from a fear of heights – there seem to be a surprisingly large number of them.

I have measured the *effort* needed to complete the walk on a scale of 1 to 4 and combined it with a *fear of heights* (if the potential exists) on a scale of A to D.

All times given for walks include a suitable allowance for rests. They are also what I feel the average reasonably fit person should be able to achieve.

On the assumption that most people cannot read complex maps but can, hopefully, read precise instructions, I've kept the maps simple and the instructions detailed. I have tried hard to omit ambiguities, but no doubt I will still get complaints from people who got lost. As

GRADING

1. An easy stroll.
2. Tiring.
3. Strenuous.
4. Exhausting and only for the very fit.

A. No exposure to heights.
B. Some mild rock scrambling, but no worse than climbing a short ladder.
C. Moderately exposed. Those with a serious fear of heights should not attempt this walk.
D. Very exposed. Not for those with even a mild fear of heights.

my Dear Old Dad used to say: When all else fails, READ THE INSTRUCTIONS.

We are indeed fortunate to live in Cape Town, where Table Mountain's craggy but serene face towers protectively over the city. I can think of no other city in the world where such natural beauty is so easily accessible. All twenty-two walks described in this book are between five and thirty minutes' drive from the city centre. The magic of Table Mountain is that after many years of walking on it, I'm *still* discovering new treasures. I sincerely hope you discover a few while reading this book.

AN HISTORICAL PEEK

Seeing the faint purple mass of Table Mountain rise from below the horizon is one of the world's great sights. The first sailor on a Dutch East Indiaman to do so was rewarded with ten guilders and six bottles of wine; and to celebrate the prospect of fresh provisions, all hands were given a tot of brandy.

The first European to climb to the top of Table Mountain was the Portuguese admiral Antonio de Saldanha in March 1503 while he and his small fleet were on their way from Lisbon to India through largely uncharted seas. For a century after that, Cape Town was known as *Agoada do Saldanha* (The Watering Place of Saldanha).

Many years later the name found its way higher up the coast by mistake: the Dutch admiral Joris van Spilbergen made a landfall 100 km to the north and assumed the sheltered bay he found there to be *Agoada do Saldanha*. Thus Saldanha Bay got its name even though the Portuguese admiral had never been there, and his original watering place became *Tafel Baay*.

In 1620 an English seafarer, Humphrey FitzHerbert, landed at what he called the Bay of Soldania (Table Bay) and in the best British tradition promptly took possession of the area in the name of his king, James I. In a short ceremony on shore he sportingly presented the bewildered Khoi with an English flag, thus making the exercise perfectly legitimate.

He then set about naming the surrounding mountains. First to be honoured was the present-day Signal Hill, which was christened 'King James His Mount'; what was later to become Lion's Head he dubbed 'Ye Sugar Loafe'. Not about to miss an opportunity to achieve everlasting fame, he named the present-day Devil's Peak 'Herbert's Mount'. Unfortunately, on his return to England, King James showed scant enthusiasm for his latest possession and it was left to the Dutch to move in.

When Jan van Riebeeck arrived in 1652 with a few more than a hundred souls, he landed at 'Leeuwenstaart' (Lion's Tail) – the present-day Granger Bay, which of course was attached to 'De Leeuwenbergh'. Herbert's Mount became Windbergh, but over five centuries and in many languages Table Mountain has always been and surely will always be Table Mountain.

SAFETY ON THE MOUNTAIN

A most revealing piece of research on mountain accidents was published in the 1987 edition of *The Journal of the Mountain Club of South Africa*. It analysed accident statistics on Table Mountain over almost the previous one hundred years, and revealed a strange paradox.

The classic rock climbs, such as Africa Crag, Africa Face, Slangolie Buttress and others, have not had one single fatality. And only one or two deaths in a hundred years have occurred on many of the other well-known difficult rock climbs. Yet it seems to be on the easy routes that people come to grief. Three deaths in Skeleton Gorge, three in Blinkwater Ravine, five in Fountain Ravine, five in Window Gorge, and even two in the almost – but evidently not quite – foolproof Platteklip Gorge.

To quote the leader article in the *Cape Times* of 8th August 1988 entitled *Easy but Deadly*, 'The lesson to be learnt from these high risk areas is the need for greater public awareness of the dangers involved. Lack of proper clothing, equipment and knowledge of the area can turn a so-called easy climb into a disasterous exercise. The foolhardy seldom venture up cliffs, but they often commit themselves with irresponsible abandon to the kloofs and gullies which even a trained climber would not attempt before taking elementary precautions. The statistics show the penalty that has all too frequently been paid.'

On that note let it be said that the author and publisher take no responsibility for any accident arising from the breaking of the following commonsense rules, or as a result of any inaccuracies which may have inadvertently crept into walk descriptions. Proceed at your own risk!

THE TEN COMMANDMENTS
OF MOUNTAIN SAFETY

(Reprinted by courtesy of the Mountain Club of South Africa)

1. Never climb alone. Four is the ideal party.
2. Choose your route according to ability, fitness and experience of the party.
3. Go with somebody who genuinely knows the way, or use a map, guidebook, or description of the route by a person who has climbed it before. Allow plenty of time to get up and down in daylight.
4. Until you know your way around, stick to the recognized routes on well-used paths. Heed signs warning of danger and do not take short cuts or negotiate unknown ravines.
5. Tell someone exactly where you are going (up and down routes and expected time of return) and stick to this plan.
6. Every party should have a leader. Keep together and travel at the pace of the slowest. Never split up and go in different directions.
7. Always go prepared for bad weather and take proper weatherproof and windproof clothing. Carry everything in a rucksack to keep arms and hands free.
8. Always watch the weather and time and turn back as soon as bad weather threatens, or if the route is no longer easy to follow.
9. Stay put in case of trouble. Don't try to force your way down in darkness or mist. Find shelter, especially from the wind.
10. If you get lost or find yourself in an area that looks unsafe, retrace your steps. Do not push on into the unknown. If you can't find the path you left, look for a safe route – preferably down broad, open slopes – making sure at all times that you can retrace your steps.

BOTANICAL FOOD FOR THOUGHT

When discussing the indigenous flora of the South-Western Cape, one important fact cannot be over-emphasised. We live in the richest floral kingdom in the world – and it's dying. Our grandchildren may never see fynbos.

The botanical world is divided into six 'floral kingdoms'. The largest is the Boreal Kingdom which covers virtually the whole of the Northern Hemisphere. The smallest in area is the Cape Floral Kingdom which stretches from Clanwilliam in the north to Grahamstown in the east along a narrow coastal strip. This tiny area is the richest of all the world's six plant kingdoms.

In the Cape Peninsula alone there are over 2 500 flowering plants – more than the whole of Britain. The whole kingdom boasts some 8 500 species – more than the entire Northern Hemisphere, three times the number of species of our nearest rival, the Amazon Basin.

Alien threat

This vast profusion of flowering plants is severely threatened by the invasion of aliens, not the least of which is mankind himself. Only 40 per cent of the fynbos flora found here in Van Riebeeck's time has survived.

Why are these aliens choking our indigenous flora? Unfortunately most have pyrophyllic seeds (pyro = fire, phyllus = love), and the intense heat of a fire stimulates the seeds to germinate, almost as if it were a signal to indicate a sudden absence of competition at ground level. Also, like any successful weed, the aliens are able to reach flowering maturity very quickly. With the exception of pines, most of the more threatening alien invaders come from Australia.

Cecil John Rhodes has been blamed for a great many things, including the introduction of Acacias to the Cape Flats in order to bind the sand, but in this case he's innocent, for there are records showing the importation of Acacia and Hakea species as early as 1833, before he was born. The blame can be laid squarely at the door of the resident botanist of the Cape Town Gardens during the 1830s, who felt there were not enough fast-growing shade trees in the Cape Colony at the time.

Unfortunately these aliens had no natural predators in South Africa and were not prone to local diseases. Being fast growers, they rapidly overcrowded the indigenous flora and in many areas replaced it with a monotonous, impenetrable green sea of one species only.

Much is done to combat the menace: for example, amateur conservation groups go out on weekend 'hacks' and cut down offending alien vegetation, but however well-meaning these groups are, I can't help feeling that they are merely scratching the surface. For every plant cut down, 100 000 seeds may be ready and waiting to germinate after the first fire. There is simply not enough manpower for 'hack groups' to succeed on more than a strictly local basis.

Nature has to be harnessed to tackle this immense threat to our environment, and this is indeed what scientists are trying to do. The invading plants are not a problem in Australia, their country of origin, because there nature provides a stabilising influence in the form of natural controls. Unfortunately when these plants were brought to the Cape, their biological governors were left behind. Currently biological control has or is being introduced to fight the Port Jackson Willow (in the form of a fungus), Hakea (fungus), Long-leafed Wattle (gall-wasp) and Blackwood (snout-beetle). Rooikrans and others are also being tackled.

But there is no instant solution. Biological controls will take a hundred years to get on top – and don't forget the countless seeds lurking below the surface. Weekend 'hacks', though, will take forever.

Blister bush

One indigenous plant to beware of is the Blister Bush, *(Peucedanum galbanum)* otherwise known as Mountain Celery because of its close resemblance and direct relationship to celery. This most interesting plant deserves healthy respect. Until very recently, little was known about the mechanism of its ability to inflict nasty blisters. Don't let anybody boast immunity because they've touched it and nothing happened – given the right set of conditions, they will blister just as badly as you and I.

Research in 1985 by Dr Natie Finkelstein of the Department of Pharmacy at UCT has cast some interesting light on this subject. It seems that a combination of slight damage or bruising to the leaves, and strong sunlight, are the essential ingredients for blisters. The compound released from the plant on bruising is not in itself harmful, but when exposed to strong ultra-violet light a change takes place in its chemical composition, which causes blistering after two days. To avoid these unpleasant blisters, the affected area should be protected from sunlight.

Two experiments by Dr Finkelstein illustrate the point. In the first an untouched branch was brushed over the left arm. The right arm was similarly treated with a branch which had been roughly handled. Only the right arm was affected. In the second experiment both arms were rubbed with bruised leaves and one arm immediately covered to exclude light. Only the exposed arm produced blisters.

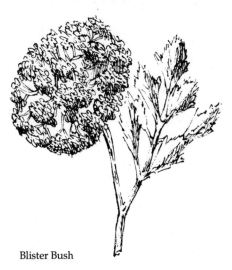

Blister Bush

BIRDS TO LOOK FOR

The rugged mountains of the Cape Peninsula, though rich in numerous plant species, do not support a wealth of bird-life. The barren rocky cliffs and exposed rocky outcrops provide little in the way of food or shelter, and it stands to reason that the few birds which are found here are well-suited to the harsh climate and habitat in which they live.

Here are the more common birds you are likely to find on your walks in the Cape Peninsula mountains. For a more complete picture and to help you correctly identify the birds, refer to *Roberts Birds of Southern Africa*; Ken Newman's *Birds of Southern Africa*; Ian Sinclair's *Field Guide to the Birds of Southern Africa;* or *Birds of the South Western Cape* by Joy Frandsen. A comprehensive list of birds recorded at Kirstenbosch is available free of charge from the National Botanic Gardens.

On the boulder-strewn upper slopes of the Table Mountain Range, look for the *Cape Rock Thrush* and the wary *Ground Woodpecker*, which abandoned life in the trees and lives on the ground. It lives in small groups and is the only terrestrial woodpecker in Africa, using tunnels excavated in earth banks in which to roost and nest.

The steep cliff faces above the contour path provide safe nesting sites for two prominent residents, the *Redwinged Starling* and the *Rock Pigeon*, which like many other starlings and pigeons have also become adapted to an urban environment. Large flocks of *Alpine* and *Black Swifts* are particularly noticeable in summer wheeling high in the sky or near the cliff faces where they nest in inaccessible vertical cracks under an overhang. These aerial birds feed on insects taken on the wing and rarely pause to rest except when breeding. The *Rock Martin*, a brown swallow-like bird, can be seen all year round in rocky and mountainous terrain where it builds its nest of mud pellets under an overhang.

Overhead look for the majestic *Black Eagle*. Although it is not all that common, there are at least four pairs resident in the Cape Peninsula. It is usually seen soaring high above the mountain crags in search of dassies which form its staple prey. Surprisingly this bird is not all black, but viewed from above it has broad white markings on the back and the rump, hence its Afrikaans name 'Witkruisarend'. Another bird of prey confined to mountainous areas is the chestnut-coloured *Rock Kestrel* which can be seen hovering in search of prey.

The *Whitenecked Raven* – a large, strong-flying bird of the mountains – is sometimes confused with the more familiar, but smaller *Pied Crow* or 'Witborskraai',as both birds have glossy black plumage with white markings. At most times of the year in the fynbos, you are likely to see the *Cape Sugarbird* which is attracted to the sweet nectar of the Protea flowers, but is also adept at hawking for insects which form an important part of its diet, especially during the breeding season. During its conspicuous undulating display flight, the male's long beak and streamer-like tail make it instantly recognisable. Another fynbos resident is the *Orangebreasted Sunbird*, which is found in stands of Proteas and Ericas in Kirstenbosch, on the top and along the western slopes of Table Mountain. The brightly-coloured male usually calls from a vantage point on a tall shrub. Other sunbirds resident in the Peninsula mountain chain are the *Lesser Doublecollared Sunbird* and the less common *Malachite Sunbird*.

Two other common residents of the fynbos and surrounding dense bush, are the *Cape Bulbul* and the *Cape Francolin*, a fairly large gamebird with mottled brown plumage and red legs. Not as easily identified is the *Grassbird* or 'lollipop bird' as it is sometimes known because of its plump chestnut-brown chest and longish tail. Look for it in long grass or skulking in bushes.

The small pockets of natural forest seldom harbour many birds. At the forest edge look for *Cape Batis, Sombre Bulbul, Olive Thrush, Dusky Flycatcher* and *Paradise Flycatcher*. In the forest canopy and in fruiting trees and large shrubs, especially along the contour path near Cecilia Forest and Kirstenbosch, the *Rameron Pigeon* is evident, while the shy *Cinnamon Dove* haunts the forest floor. A forest bird more often heard than seen is the *Redchested Cuckoo* or Piet-my-vrou, a summer migrant which mainly parasitises the nests of the *Cape Robin*.

Finally a word about LBJs – little brown jobs – which are those drab brown birds that are almost impossible to identify unless you are an expert birder. LBJs (or 'tinktinkies' as they are commonly called in Afrikaans) are generally beautiful songsters – how else can they hope to attract a mate? LBJs to look for include the *Cape Bunting, Cape Siskin* – a canary-like bird found in pairs or small parties feeding on seeds and insects, *Familiar Chat* – found on rock outcrops, *Greybacked Cisticola, Neddicky* and *Karoo Prinia*.

Cape Sugarbird

SNAKES IN PERSPECTIVE

Snakes must be among the most misunderstood and unfairly maligned of all God's creatures. They are commonly regarded as vermin which should be killed on sight, yet they occupy a most important niche in the ecosystem. The balance of nature would be severely upset without any control on the population of rats, mice and other pests.

While the danger of a small number of snake species must never be underestimated, I do believe that the threat of death from snakebite while walking on the mountain should be put firmly in perspective. In South Africa an average of 15 people die each year as a result of snakebite, with most fatalities occurring in Northern Zululand. Yet a survey in Natal in 1978 revealed that only one in

Cape Cobra

every 68 recorded snakebites resulted in death. By comparison over 200 people are struck dead by lightning every year; 10 000 people die in the carnage on our roads; and 29 000 die as a result of smoking-related diseases. If *you* are a smoker, you can stop worrying about being bitten by a dangerous snake. What you are doing is about 2000 times more likely to kill you!

There are some 23 snake species in the Cape Peninsula, of which only five are dangerous. There are about 130 species in Southern Africa, 14 of them deadly. It therefore follows that should you come across a snake on the mountain, as I do perhaps once or twice a year, the chances are that it does not deserve the fate you probably wish upon it. However, it would be foolhardy to regard any snake with contempt. In the Cape Peninsula the five that need to be given a wide berth are the Puff Adder, Berg Adder, Cape Cobra, Rinkhals and Boomslang.

The venom injected by most dangerous snakes falls into three categories. The Cape Peninsula's 'fearsome five' includes all three types:
Cytotoxic venom is a tissue-destroying poison which causes serious localised swelling, inflammation and eventual kidney failure due to fluid loss. Puff Adder venom is extremely cytotoxic.
Neurotoxic venom attacks the nervous system serving the diaphragm, chest and throat muscles and death is by asphyxiation. The Cape Cobra, Rinkhals and Berg Adder fall into this category.

However, no deaths have been attributed to the Berg Adder. *Haemotoxic venom* contains enzymes which activate the body's clotting mechanism, resulting in minute but fatal blood clots throughout the body and consequently a great loss of usable blood. The Boomslang delivers haemotoxic venom, although fatal bites are rare due to its non-aggressive nature.

The deadliest of snakes in Southern Africa is the Black Mamba of the Natal coast, Northern Transvaal and parts of Namibia. Fortunately it is not found in the South-Western Cape. The Boomslang is a close second, but the incidence of fatalities accredited to these snakes is relatively low. More deaths result from Puff Adder bites than any other in Southern Africa, not because of the strength of the venom, but rather due to the high incidence of bites. However in the Cape Province, it is the Cape Cobra which holds this dubious distinction.

SNAKE MYTHS

A few fallacies about snakes that need to be exploded are:

☐ Snakes do not travel in pairs. They are loners and only pair off briefly to mate.

☐ Snakes do not hypnotise their prey.

☐ Snakes are not deliberately aggressive. They strike in self-defence if trodden on or unexpectedly disturbed. They do not chase after people.

☐ Death from an untreated Black Mamba bite occurs within 7-15 hours, not five minutes as is commonly believed.

☐ Puff Adders do not strike backwards, nor do any other snakes for that matter.

☐ Most snakes will get out of your way first. Unfortunately this does not apply to the Puff Adder, which accounts for its high incidence of bites.

SNAKE BITE FIRST AID
DO'S AND DONT'S

1. Apply a firm pressure bandage over the bitten area and immobilise the limb. Do *not* use a tourniquet, as most venom is now thought to be carried by the lymphatic system and not in the bloodstream. The application of a tourniquet increases the possibility of gangrene, especially in the case of a Puff Adder bite.
2. Do not cut the bitten area; rather use an 'Aspervenin' suction pump kit, obtainable from most hiking shops.
3. Do not inject antivenom. This should be left to a doctor. Injection of the incorrect antivenom, or any antivenom at all if the victim hasn't been poisoned, could itself cause death.
4. Do not hunt down the snake and attempt to kill it, as a second bite would really complicate matters.
5. If the victim shows difficulty in breathing, apply artificial respiration until medical assistance is obtained.
6. Do not give the victim alcohol.
7. Above all, remember that snakebite deaths are extremely rare. Remain calm and reassure the victim – he could even have been bitten by a non-poisonous snake. Get the victim to medical care as soon as possible and treat symptomatically. Symptoms may not develop for 24 hours or more.
8. In the case of spitting snakes, such as the Rinkhals, do not rub the eyes, but flush with water, milk, beer, cooldrink, even urine and shade from bright light. The pain and inflamation usually subside within 24 hours.
9. Never assume that a snake is dead: a Rinkhals is an expert at feigning death and will even roll over onto its back. Adders will also remain motionless, even when provoked; therefore never pick up what at first sight appears to be a dead snake.

As in the case of mushrooms, stay well clear of snakes
if you are not an expert.

THE GEOLOGY OF THE CAPE PENINSULA

The Cape Peninsula and its mountains are composed of three rock masses of different ages. Cape Town, Signal Hill and Sea Point constitute a mass of tilted *Malmesbury Slates*, which can clearly be seen along the Atlantic shoreline of this area. The upper cliffs of *Table Mountain Sandstone*, with some slate, form the mountain masses of the Cape Peninsula, and these rest on a solid foundation of *Cape Granite*, which can be most clearly seen as huge rounded boulders on the slopes of Lion's Head and on either side of the coastal road from Camps Bay to Hout Bay and below Chapman's Peak Drive. As each formation is geologically quite different from the others, it is interesting to note how each was formed.

The *Malmesbury Slates* represent the oldest formation in the Cape Peninsula. They were deposited as muddy sediments in a body of water over a long period about 800 million years ago. Subsequently, by the effects of heat and pressure, they were altered into slatey rocks which earth movements tilted steeply, as can be seen in the rock ridges jutting into the sea along the beachfront at Sea Point.

The *Cape Granite* is a rock mass which crystallised out from molten magma originating from the inner part of the earth. Granite is not uniform in appearance, but has three main components, namely large crystals of grey-white felspar, with lesser amounts of glassy quartz and black specks of mica. Incidentally, the predominant felspar decays to form clay, including the kaolin deposits being quarried between Fish Hoek and Noordhoek.

The *Table Mountain Sandstone* is sedimentary rock, meaning it was formed by millions of years of river-borne sediment which piled up on itself and was compressed by its own weight. If one looks carefully at sandstone cliffs, it will be noticed that they form large rectangular blocks. This is because the rock was laid down in horizontal beds which later became vertically fractured because of the horizontal movements of the earth's crust. The subsequent erosion of these rocks by wind, rain and glacial action resulted in the formation of ledges, vertical cliffs and flat table tops.Ever since they were lifted out of the primeval waters, the natural forces of weathering have been eroding at the Table Mountain Sandstone mass. What we see today is only the remnant of this great accumulation of sediments. Geologically speaking Table Mountain is in the winter of its life: the continued erosion will cause the mass to be flattened to the level of the present Cape Flats.

AGE OF TABLE MOUNTAIN

The rocks that make up Table Mountain are about 600 million years old, but as a raised geological feature the mountain is only a maximum of 60 million years old, compared to the age of the planet, which is 4 600 million years. The age of Table Mountain may be difficult to imagine, but it is easier to comprehend major events in relation to one another if we concertina these 4 600 million years into one calendar year.

- [ ] During the entire January and half of February the earth supports no life at all. It is an inorganic planet in the process of cooling.
- [ ] About 17 February simple microbes form.
- [ ] On 4 March the earliest known sedimentary rocks form.
- [ ] On 3 September the continents start drifting apart and the first mountains are formed by folding.
- [ ] On 13 November animals evolve hard shells.
- [ ] On 29 November vertebrates evolve and the earth is clothed in plant life.
- [ ] On 7 December coal is deposited.
- [ ] On 15 December oxygen reaches present levels.
- [ ] On 22 December dinosaurs rule the earth and the present-day continents begin to separate.
- [ ] On 25 December a cataclysmic event causes the extinction of many species, including the dinosaurs.
- [ ] On 26 December the precursor of Table Mountain, at least six times its present height, is formed.
- [ ] On 28 December the Himalayas begin to form.
- [ ] On 31 December at 20h00 primitive man first sets foot on the planet. Christ is born at 14 seconds to midnight and the Industrial Revolution begins a second before the year ends.
- [ ] Immense geological changes take place on the last day of our compressed year. As recently as 4 minutes to midnight on 31 December the whole of False Bay is dry land.

THE WEATHER

The climate of the South-Western Cape is described in the geography books as 'Mediterranean'. By definition this describes long, warm summers and short, mild winters with the rainfall occurring mainly in winter. We share this climate with California and South-Western Australia, apart from the Mediterranean region itself.

However, the South-Western Cape and in particular the Cape Peninsula differs markedly from the other regions in that our weather is notoriously unpredictable: being a weatherman in Cape Town must be a most frustrating profession. There is only one foolproof weathervane in the Cape Peninsula: when there is cloud on Lion's Head and nowhere else, rain is guaranteed within the next 12 hours.

I have often started up the mountain under clear blue skies and balmy weather, only to come down a few hours later in pouring rain accompanied by a chilling wind. Visitors to the Cape, in particular, should be warned never to underestimate the weather, as it can change dramatically in just half an hour. Locals should know better, but I have often found inexperienced hikers adrift in the cold wind and rain, dressed only in T-shirts and shorts.

Regardless of the weather when you start, always take raingear and warm clothes. It is also advisable to take a hat and a waterbottle.

Lion's Head

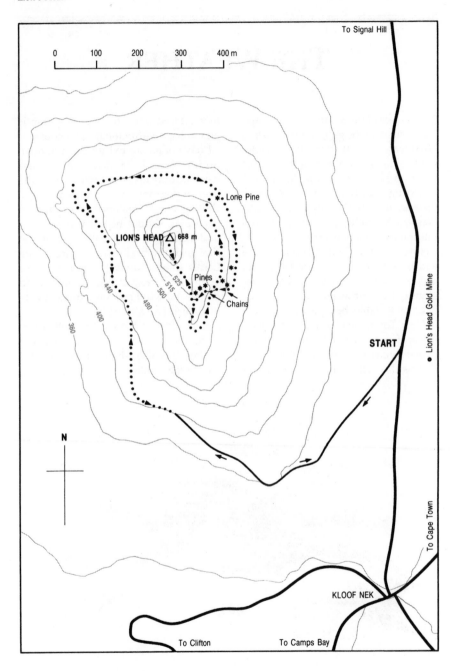

LION'S HEAD

1

Time: $2\frac{1}{2}$ *hours*
Grade: *2C or 2B, depending on the route*
Water: *None available*

This is probably the best value-for-energy walk in the Cape Peninsula. For the minimum of effort you are treated to a kaleidoscope of views as you spiral your way to the top.

Originally called Sugar Loaf, I was fascinated to learn that Lion's Head actually had its very own gold mine. Following so-called expert advice, a company, not surprisingly called the Lion's Head Gold Mining Syndicate, was formed in 1887 and actually sank a shaft some 30 m deep about 100 m below the tar road, at the beginning of this walk. This was no mere arbitrary scratching of the surface. Some gold quartz was said to have been found and in no time at all Lion's Head was teeming with prospective millionaires. Needless to say, the gold rush soon fizzled out when tests showed the quantities to be uneconomical. Imagine, though, if it had proved to be worthwhile. With beautiful scenery, wine, oil *and* gold, we Kaapenaars would perhaps have become even more arrogant and independent than ever in the eyes of our Vaalie friends!

But enough of this daydreaming, let's get on with our walk. If you do not have your own transport, take a bus to Kloof Nek. Once there, take the road up to Signal Hill and follow it for 600-700 m until you come to a parking area on either side of the road. This is your starting point up a gravel road closed off with a chain which passes through a most impressive stand of Silver Trees *(Leucadendron argenteum)*. I can't think of anywhere else where they are so concentrated. And remember, they grow nowhere else in the world, but on the slopes of Table Mountain. These fickle trees are a majestic sight in a gentle breeze, their leaves shimmering and glinting. Also growing in great profusion here, perhaps more than in most places, is the Blister Bush *(Peucedanum galbanum)*. Fortunately they're well off the road and not likely to bother you.

Notice Molteno Reservoir on your left as you start: not that long ago this little birdbath provided all of Cape Town's water supply. The diagonal line of large pine trees on the cliff face above you more or less marks your route after you have completed the first circuit.

After fifteen minutes the road narrows to a wide path, and you enjoy a kaleidoscope of views as you spiral around the mountain: first the City Bowl, then Camps Bay, closely followed by Clifton and Sea Point and then the Mother City once again. You might be surprised at how green and tree-lined Fresnaye (upper Sea Point) is. One doesn't tend to notice it from ground level.

About 10 minutes after the road narrows to a path, you'll come to a fork. Keep to the upper right-hand path, as the left fork leads down to Lion's Rump (Signal Hill) and Sea Point. At this point, look down to the coast and notice two rocky outcrops forcing their way through the breakers off Clifton. These are called rather quaintly North Paw and South Paw (of the Lion).

Once around the corner, look down onto the Lion's Rump and notice the kramat or Muslim tomb, one of many dotted about the Peninsula. This one is the final resting place of Hassan Ghaibe Sha Al Quadri, an Islamic leader. Soon you'll come to a large pine tree in the path, just as Molteno Reservoir comes back into view. Carry on along the level, despite a few tempting paths leading upwards, and after 200 m you'll come to a second large pine tree in the pathway. Just beyond it you'll find the first set of chains that will help you to climb the rock face. You've now done a complete circuit of the mountain.

Don't be put off by the chains. The way up is not difficult, even if you do have a fear of heights. The chains are really cosmetic, rather like Linus' blanket for those who need reassuring. If, however, you have a serious fear of heights, see the end of this chapter, and the map, for an alternative route.

Kramat on Signal Hill

Scramble up the 8-m chain, then immediately up another, shorter chain. (Don't worry, they are well secured.) Now climb the steep slope immediately above: a third and fourth chain help you. Then follow the four pines diagonally up to the left. At the last pine, double back up the ridge, using a 3-m ladder. From the ladder it looks like heavy going, but it's only another 10 minutes to the top. And when you get there – what a panorama! Looking down the length of the Lion's Rump (Signal Hill), it is not too difficult to imagine the breakwater being the lion's tail.

At night under a full moon this climb is sheer magic. Why not try it around sunset and get the best of both worlds?

TO AVOID THE CHAINS (ALTERNATIVE ROUTE)

A few metres before the first large pine in the pathway going up Lion's Head, a path goes steeply up to the right. This traverses across the face between the second and third chains, continues around the ridge and up to just above the diagonal line of pines, and hence to the ladder. When returning from the top, just keep going straight on after climbing down the ladder, i.e. don't double back at the pines. It also makes a welcome change to come down this way.

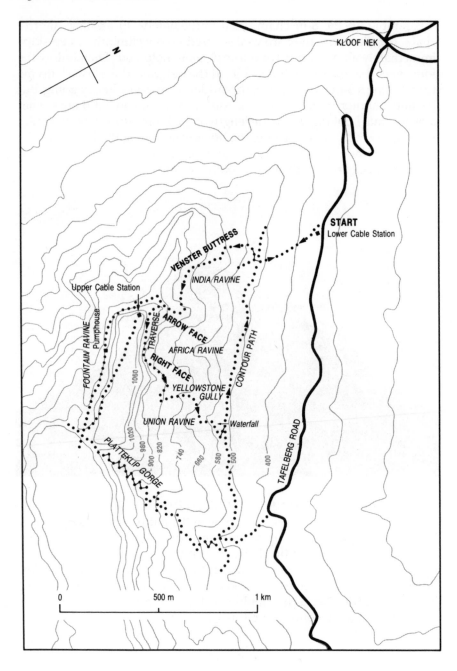

RIGHT FACE – ARROW FACE TRAVERSE

2

Time: $4\frac{1}{2}$ *hours*
Grade: *4D (This route is for experienced mountaineers only)*
Water: *Available on Africa Ledge only*

This is surely the most remarkable walk on Table Mountain: extremely exposed on the traverse, yet still just a walk with a couple of tricky rock scrambles. It's really no more difficult than walking along a narrow pavement, excepting that the gutter is about a hundred metres below!

If you have a fear of heights, stay away from this one; but if you are fit and can handle the exposure, then this walk presents you with a stiff but interesting slog up, followed by an exhilarating traverse along a ledge which on two occasions seems to come to a dead end – only to continue *inside* the mountain where the face of the mountain has literally shifted forward to leave a corridor behind for you to squeeze through.

If you study the photomap, you will notice that this climb doesn't go to the top of Table Mountain. However, if you want to do this, perhaps preferring to come down by cable car, then take the optional extra described at the end of the chapter.

Start at the Lower Cable Station. Facing the mountain, you will see some steps at the right-hand side of the parking area. Take them and soon you will be following the cable car up some steep rock steps. Within 15 to 20 minutes you should reach the contour path, where you will be confronted by a notice announcing 'This route is considered dangerous. Inexperienced climbers should use Platteklip Route'.

Disregard this ominous sign (though you have been warned) and cross straight over the contour path. Take the right-hand option where the path forks 10 m further on. (The left fork follows the route of the cable car up India Ravine, which is a more difficult alternative to the one we are following.) Your way up is called India-Venster Route. India Ravine is the one the cableway follows up and Venster Buttress is to the right of it. Your route is a combination of both. India Ravine gets its name from the fact that, viewed from the city, it takes on the outline of a map of India. Venster Buttress has a picturesque 'venster' (window) in the rocks, which we shall see some 10 to 15 minutes after leaving the contour path. If you wish to make a slight detour to the window, keep an eye open for a pile of boulders on the skyline 100 m to the left and 10 to 15 minutes above the contour path, whilst in a narrow gully. Get above the line of the boulders, then leave the path to get to the 'venster' about 100 m to the left. It frames Devil's Peak beautifully from one side and Lion's Head from the other.

Once back on the path, continue the upward slog for another 10 minutes before emerging from the gully. Ahead and to the left you will see the top of India Ravine. Your route traverses the top of India Ravine and goes diagonally up to the top left-hand corner, after which a short rock scramble (more or less straight up) is necessary. Follow the path, and keep a sharp eye open for cairns and foot-worn rock.

Once over the rock scramble, follow the cairns in the direction of the Upper Cable Station. You will reach a spot where the path takes you to almost directly below the cable station; at the same time there is a short, sheer cliff face on your right. This is an important junction. On the face of Table Mountain in front and to the left of you are three bushy ledges. The middle one is Africa Ledge and the lower one Right Face – Arrow Face Traverse. Just as the path starts climbing steeply up to Africa Ledge, a faint path goes down to the left. This is your way.

If you decide to take the optional extra (see end of chapter) to the Upper Cable Station, then this is the point to which you must return, so as to ascend to the higher level of Africa Ledge.

For the time being, however, you descend slightly to Right Face – Arrow Face Traverse. After about 7 minutes the precipitous path apparently comes to an abrupt end. Closer inspection of the rock face will reveal a narrow crack: get into it and walk 8 m behind the face of the mountain. On emerging into the sunlight again, immediately turn right and scramble 2 m up onto a higher ledge. After walking 25 m along this ledge, you again run out of space. Squeeze through a narrow crack into another tunnel which is closed overhead for 20 m and then becomes an open corridor for another 30 m. At this point scramble down 3 to 4 m at the very end of the ledge near a rocky cairn.

Now follow the clear path for about 100 m, but don't let it take you to a rocky corner: you must drop down to a lower level about 25 m before reaching the corner. Cairns mark the down route to a level some 10 m below. This lower path will now lead you safely around the corner into the top of Yellowstone Gully. Follow the cairns down.

Once over a short rock scramble, turn left and head straight down. Do not continue the traverse. Keep a sharp lookout for cairns, because

if you lose them, then you are lost! If this happens, retrace your steps to the last cairn and look again. Yellowstone Gully goes straight down for a distance, then turns sharp right into Union Ravine. Traverse halfway across Union Ravine to reach the river bed, and then continue on down. Beware, however: 5 minutes down Union Ravine you need to cross the river, allowing the path to take you the 100 m across and to the other side before descending to the contour path. If you were to continue down the river bed, you could just walk off into space!

About 15 minutes' walk along the contour path will complete your circuit under the cableway. Continue down to the Lower Cable Station to complete this exciting walk.

In case you have any misgivings about the cableway, it was officially opened on 4 October 1929, and at the time of writing has carried some 8 million passengers with not a single accident. I once told this to a rather nervous overseas visitor, who accused me of tempting fate! The cable is visually inspected and lubricated once a month, and once every six months an electromagnetic rope test is done.

Had the Cape Town City Council carried out their plans before World War I, a funicular railway would have been built up Fountain Ravine. However, the sterling work of Norwegian engineer Trygve Stromsoe gave us the very safe and highly successful cableway which carries up to 28 passengers to the summit in only 5 minutes.

AFRICA LEDGE TO THE UPPER CABLE STATION (Optional Extra)

Time: *45 minutes one way*
Grade: *2C*
Water: *Available*

Having returned to the spot mentioned earlier, climb up to the level of Africa Ledge and take the path around the corner to the right overlooking Camps Bay. Five minutes further on you will come to a rock scramble which goes straight up (the path will no longer continue its traverse to the right). About 50 m higher up, the path continues its right traverse at the higher level. Some 5 minutes after reaching the top of the rock scramble, the narrow path passes centimetres away from the highest sheer drop on Table Mountain. You are now entering Fountain Ravine, which may be picturesque, but is narrow and pretty hairy.

Soon a concrete pumphouse will come into view. After stepping over a metal water pipe which takes water from the pumphouse to the restaurant on the mountain, scramble up the rock face opposite on the left: the route is clear. Alternatively carry on up Fountain Ravine (the 'fountain' is where the pumphouse gets the water it pumps). The pumphouse was built in 1928 to raise water the last 60 m to the construction site of the Upper Cable Station. The top of Fountain Ravine meets up with the back of Platteklip Gorge, which is the gap in the middle of the table as seen from the city.

Either way, the route to the Upper Cable Station is obvious. Refreshments await you in the restaurant, if you can fight your way through all the tourists!

THE PIPE TRACK 3

Time: *3 hours*
Grade: *1A*
Water: *None available in summer*

This is a most pleasant stroll and not at all strenuous, although in summer it is recommended that you do this walk in the early morning when most of it is still in shade. It will take about $1\frac{1}{2}$ hours to get to Slangolie Ravine where the Pipe Track ends, and slightly less time getting back. It is one of the best-known hikes in Cape Town, and certainly one of the oldest, for the Pipe Track was constructed in 1887 to lay the pipeline from the proposed reservoirs on Table Mountain to Kloof Nek. Work began in the same year on the Woodhead Tunnel to which the track leads.

The start of this walk is at Kloof Nek, next to the fire hazard board. Follow the steps up alongside the neatly trimmed hedge surrounding the waterworks' cottage. I wonder if anyone has bothered to tell the occupant that the hedge is Australian myrtle, a dreaded alien invader!

At the top of the steps you'll see Camps Bay and get a first look at the pipe where it crosses a small ravine. This first aqueduct is known as the Blockhouse Aqueduct after a long since demolished blockhouse and gun battery built in 1781 by the French. Believe it or not, the French occupied the Cape for about eighteen months to protect the Dutch settlers against the English. The French it seems, would travel half the world to have a pot shot at the Poms.

Note the occasional benches at strategic viewpoints. You are so close to the city and yet the feeling of unspoilt nature and raw mountain are all around you. I've been fortunate enough to have travelled widely, but can think of no other large city with such easy access to nature and breathtaking views. Rio de Janeiro, Sydney and Vancouver might not agree, but they don't hold a candle to Cape Town.

The second aqueduct is appropriately named Granite Aqueduct. Discourage your children (and some adults) from trying to do a tight-rope act on the pipe. It could spoil your entire day!

Ten to fifteen minutes after starting you will find yourself below the Kloof Nek Filtration Plant. Built in 1938 to treat the water from Woodhead Reservoir, it gave Cape Town its first crystal-clear water. Prior to

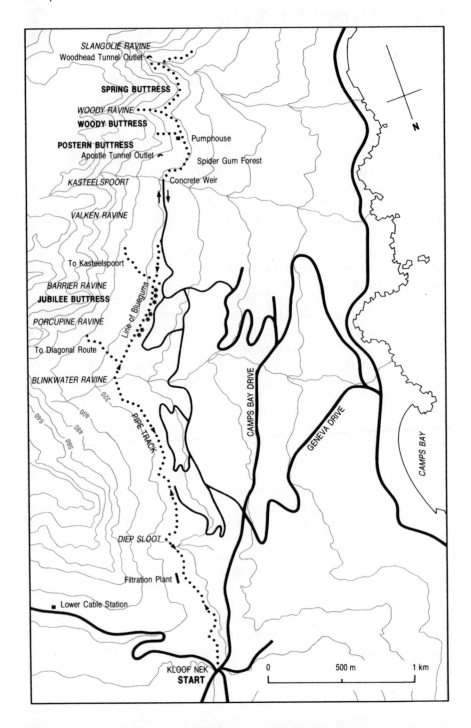

1938 the water that came from Cape Town taps was brown. Looking up at the imposing building, notice the cannon, probably a relic from the French visitation.

Beyond the filtration plant the Pipe Track plunges down into Diep Sloot, giving you some work to do getting up the other side. This is really the greatest effort you have to put in on the whole journey, which generally follows a level contour for most of the way. Every so often you will come across a small brick-and-cement housing containing a valve. They have recently been numbered, which makes a description of the route easier. At 'Air Valve 7' (about 25 minutes after leaving Kloof Nek) look up at the Upper Cable Station, an imposing structure built in 1929. The big gap to the right is Blinkwater Ravine. At 'Air Valve 12' look up and see the deep cut immediately to the right of the cable station. This is Fountain Ravine. It's difficult to imagine that there is a path up there (see Chapter 2), coming across from the left where the cable cuts across the skyline. It is even more difficult to think that the Cape Town Municipality contemplated routing a track railway for tourists up there before the cableway method was finally settled on.

You should reach the bottom of Blinkwater Ravine 40 to 45 minutes after leaving Kloof Nek. After a serious rockfall a few years ago the ravine was closed to the public. A fence closing off the original path can be seen at the end of another aqueduct crossing the Blinkwater Stream. Its original name was Stinkwater, but now it seems to have been upgraded, even if it is closed.

Two minutes beyond the base of Blinkwater Ravine, a rocky cairn marks the start of Diagonal Route, which goes up to the left. This is covered in Chapter 4. Carry on along the Pipe Track past weatherbeaten and fire-ravaged bluegums until, 10 minutes beyond Blinkwater Ravine, you reach a signpost indicating another important route up to the Back Table, namely Kasteelspoort (meaning Castle's Gateway). Again keep on the level. Five minutes later a jeep track joins your path from the right-hand quarter. This is a relic from the construction of the Apostles Tunnel in 1964. Remember this jeep track, for it is an alternative route down provided you have left a car at the top of Camps Bay, thus saving you 45 minutes on the return trip.

Beyond 'Air Valve 17' look past the three large pine trees ahead and pick out a straight scar going directly up the mountain for about 100 m. This leads to the outlet of Apostles Tunnel, which replaced Woodhead Tunnel in 1964.

About one hour after starting you should cross a concrete weir which in winter is usually overflowing with water cascading down Kasteelspoort. Look up and see the 'Castle's Gateway'. A sign decrees that there shall be no overnight camping, which is a classic bit of Councilese bureaucracy. I cannot imagine anything more uncomfortable than camping on a concrete weir.

The road peters out here as there is no further need for it. The gravel path ascends gently and on the hilltop the trig beacon atop Slangolie Buttress comes into view, as well as an exceptionally solidly built pumphouse which looks more like a mausoleum. Fifteen metres beyond the mausoleum-like pumphouse is the turn-off up Woody Buttress, a very popular and easy rock climb. Five minutes on will bring you to the base of Woody Ravine, a steep and narrow route to the top. A further 5 minutes will take you around the corner and into Slangolie Ravine. Your path is up a series of steep steps clinging to the side of the ravine. Note the very loose scree high up in the ravine: only the indigenous forest at the top seems to be keeping the rest of the rocks from tumbling down.

A rusty notice a little further on warns of a 'Dangerous Ascent'. About a minute beyond the rusty notice the path is hemmed in on both sides by Buchu bushes. Take the tiny leaves between finger and thumb and crush them: the pleasant smell will remain with you all day.

Soon you'll come to a second but much newer notice, once again warning of a 'Dangerous Ascent'. This one is much more relevant than the first. I have climbed up Slangolie Ravine, but it is a case of two steps forward and one back, as the loose rock is indeed dangerous. At this new 'Dangerous Ascent' notice, a path goes upwards and downwards. Go down if you need water and up if you insist on going to the very end of the Pipe Track 5 minutes further along. The up bit isn't dangerous as long as you stop when you reach a small cave and gate marked 'Danger'. Beyond this you need ropes to get to the opening of the Woodhead Tunnel. Do not proceed beyond the gate. The tunnel is closed off with iron bars anyway, so it is not worth the risk.

Despite its lurking dangers and ominous name, Slangolie Ravine is peaceful and tranquil, and is also a haven for indigenous trees.

Perhaps returning the same way doesn't appeal to you, but somehow it is different. Anyway, you should be able to do it in about 15 minutes less than the outward journey.

VALLEY OF THE RED GODS

4

Time: $3\frac{1}{2}$ hours (add an hour extra to the Valley of Isolation)
Grade: 3C
Water: Available

This is one of my favourite walks up one of the most popular routes on Table Mountain (Kasteelspoort) and down a cliffhanger with spectacular views (Diagonal Route). At the terminus there are a couple of lush box canyons to choose from for your rest and tea break.

Start by driving to the very top of Rontree Estate, above Camps Bay. Turn off Camps Bay Drive into Fiskaal Road, which leads into Francolin Avenue and eventually to Theresa Avenue. At the highest point of Theresa Avenue a little side road leads to a gate and a Table Mountain Nature Reserve signpost. Park your car here, being careful not to block anyone's driveway.

Walk up the concrete strip road beyond the gate for about ten minutes, after which time you will come to a fork. Keep right at the fork. You want to reach the line of tall bluegums above you, as these mark the contour of the Pipe Track. A hundred paces past the fork, leave the strip road up some rock steps to the left heading directly upwards towards the bluegums. On reaching the Pipe Track (and the bluegums), you should be confronted by a metal signpost pointing the way up Kasteelspoort. You should have reached this point within about 15 minutes of leaving your car. If you run out of concrete strip road, you have overshot the mark. Remember the bluegums.

The signpost marks the beginning of one of the most popular routes up Table Mountain, leading to the Back Table, Mountain Club huts and the reservoirs. Kasteelspoort (meaning Castle's Gate) is affectionately known to aficionados simply as 'KP'. From here it should take $1\frac{1}{4}$ to $1\frac{1}{2}$ hours to reach the top of KP, depending on how fit and keen you are.

The path starts climbing gradually, becoming steeper and steeper as it cuts diagonally up across the slope for about half an hour before traversing along the level for 100 m. Then comes a sharp incline before you reach a large, wide slab, which is a welcome spot for a rest despite the marks left by the sick graffiti brigade.

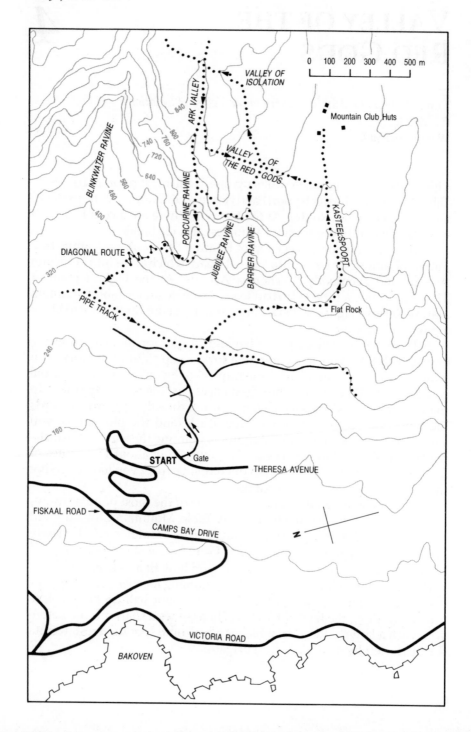

After your rest, you start the steep climb up and around the corner into Kasteelspoort itself, and should soon see how appropriate the name is. About half an hour after leaving the 'slab' you are finally at the top, marked by a metal signpost showing you two ways: Skeleton Gorge and Maclear's Beacon straight ahead (both a long way off) and Spring to the left. The 'Spring' referred to is in the Valley of the Red Gods, so left is your route. You need to head for the gap in the mountains in the direction indicated by the Spring sign. Keep left at a slight fork, 50 m from the sign. Five minutes later you should be over the ridge and into the Valley of the Red Gods, a small but pretty valley closed in on all sides. In the middle of it you will come to another metal sign pointing to the right, indicating the direction of Platteklip Gorge.

This is the point at which you have a choice. Depending on how much time you have left, you can either start for home, or be a little more adventurous and return to this spot via two adjoining valleys. These are the Valley of Isolation and Ark Valley. The former is particularly pretty, with a waterfall which disappears into a cavern in the ground, and at the end of Ark Valley, one of the most spectacular views on Table Mountain awaits you. Your return journey from here to your car will take about $1\frac{1}{4}$ to $1\frac{1}{2}$ hours without the optional extra which is described at the end of this chapter.

From the Platteklip Gorge sign, you need to reach the western lip of the valley in order to take the Diagonal Route back down towards home. It is so named because it traverses diagonally across three ravines and three buttresses before depositing you back onto the Pipe Track. Once at the lip on the seaward side of the Valley of the Red Gods, the path descends steeply down Barrier Ravine. Just before the 'barrier' – a sheer drop preventing further descent – the path swings to the right, drops down a bit and then traverses across the top of Jubilee Ravine along a precipitous path.

It then continues into Porcupine Ravine, a deep gully through which you follow the steep path down, once again swinging to the right before running out of terra firma. Enjoy the spectacular view of Bakoven framed by Jubilee and Porcupine buttresses. The path skirts around Porcupine Buttress along a wide bushy ledge, then drops 4 m down a mild rock scramble. Just at the end of the bushy ledge and 20 m before the down scramble, note Porcupine Cave on the right. It hardly justifies the 'cave' description, for it is really no more than a rock overhang. At the base of the rock scramble turn right, even though a path seems to go off to the left. After this part the path zigzags all the way down to the Pipe Track. Once on the Pipe Track, turn left and proceed for 5 or 6 minutes to a point where you are well into the line of bluegums at which you started. You don't need to go all the way back to the start of Kasteelspoort; instead take a shortcut down at a fire hydrant point marked by a black-and-yellow striped pole. Fifty metres below the Pipe Track you will come across a gravel road. Turn left and soon you will be on the concrete road on which you came up. Your car is just a few minutes away.

VALLEY OF ISOLATION (OPTIONAL EXTRA)

This is well worth an extra 45 to 60 minutes if you have the time.

Leave the Platteklip sign in the Valley of the Red Gods and proceed in the direction it indicates along a path which heads up the valley just *before* the sign (backtrack a few metres). An upward climb of 10 to 15 minutes will get you to the lip between the Valley of the Red Gods and the Valley of Isolation. The latter is a deeper and more 'boxed in' valley which, apart from befitting its name, is rich in unspoilt fynbos, especially King Proteas, Geelbos and Volstruisies. Its main feature is a grotto which for most of the year has a modest but pleasant waterfall cascading into it. As a youngster, I used to camp in this superb little spot but, alas, overnight camping is no longer permitted on Table Mountain.

After you have sampled the crystal waters of the grotto, continue on the path to about halfway up the far side of the valley, before it swings northward, passing some interesting caves on the left, and leads over the top and into Ark Valley. At the top of Isolation, look back and see Hout Bay Harbour in the distance with the Sentinel towering protectively over it. And beyond that, Kommetjie Beach and the Lighthouse.

The path drops gently into Ark Valley, a shallow and narrow cutting which runs in an East/West direction. At its base, cross the perennial stream and about 5 m on, turn left. Were you to carry straight on and up, you would finish up at Platteklip. But that is not your way.

To the left down Ark Valley will take you through wet marshy ground – especially in winter – for about 5 minutes. Just as the path starts to descend gently, an indistinct path branches off to the left through Restios or thatching reeds and up through the weathered grey rocks. If the path starts to descend steeply down Porcupine Ravine, and you can see the coastline of Camps Bay, you have gone too far. Retrace your steps about 100 m and look for that indistinct way through the rocks.

Just a few metres up, above the rocks, on the ridge, you will find a path heading westwards towards the sea. Follow it for 3 minutes almost to the end of the buttress, and you will find a clear path going down to the left, following a firebreak, back into the Valley of the Red Gods. The view from this point is quite breathtaking. Five minutes down the firebreak will bring you back to the Platteklip sign at which you started this worthwhile detour.

View of Lion's Head

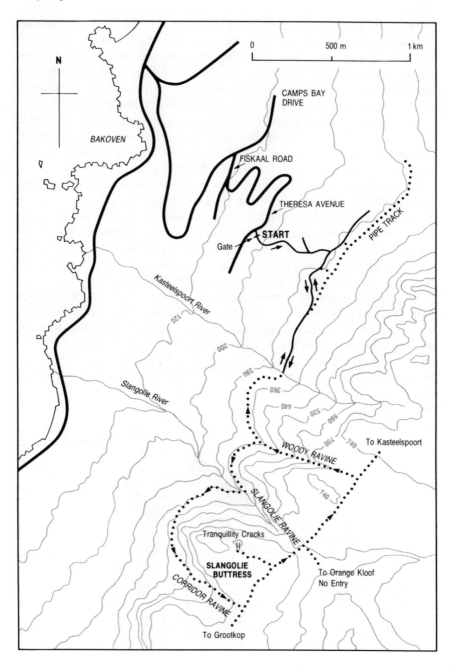

TRANQUILLITY CRACKS 5

Time: *4 hours*
Grade: *3C*
Water: *Available on the lower slopes*

This was one of Table Mountain's best kept secrets. In recent years, however, I have noticed that the path to this gem has become more and more well used. The 1987 issue of the *Journal of the Mountain Club of South Africa* finally let the cat out of the bag and Tranquillity Cracks were on the map. Also known as Yellowwood Cracks and The Underground Forest, it is a fascinating trick of nature which from above looks like metre-high fynbos – but what you're seeing from above is the tip of the iceberg, so to speak. Below the tip is a veritable forest of Yellowwoods growing from a crack in the skull of Table Mountain.

Situated on the crest of Slangolie Buttress, Tranquillity Cracks are best reached by going up Corridor Ravine and returning via Woody Ravine. Start by driving to the very top of Rontree Estate, above Camps Bay. Turn off Camps Bay Drive into Fiskaal Road, which leads into Francolin Avenue and eventually Theresa Avenue. At the highest point of Theresa Avenue a little side road leads to a gate and a Table Mountain Nature Reserve signpost. Park your car here, being careful not to block anyone's driveway. Walk up the jeep track beyond the gate, keeping to the right all the way until you reach the Pipe Track (see Chapter 3). Now you're on the level, and soon the track narrows to a path and ascends gently. At the hilltop, notice the trig beacon atop Slangolie Buttress. This marks the spot very close to your destination. You soon pass a pumphouse which looks like a mausoleum but which more than anything is a lasting monument to the skill of the Scottish stonemasons who constructed the reservoirs on Table Mountain over a century ago.

Five minutes past the pumphouse you will come to a notice indicating Woody Ravine. This marks the end of your down route. Keep following the Pipe Track and soon you will round the corner into Slangolie Ravine. The path climbs some steep steps clinging to the side of the ravine. A rusty notice soon proclaims 'Dangerous Ascent'. Ignore it, because you are not, for the time being anyway, going up. Soon you'll come to a second but much newer notice, once again warning 'Dangerous Ascent'. This time take it seriously and go down to the river bed. Cross over the stony rivercourse (dry for most of the year) and follow the path which continues on the other side of the ravine. After passing under a rock face, it picks its way steeply up the slope under dense indigenous trees. Five minutes after leaving the Slangolie river bed, the path levels out into a rock overhang. From here on the path is quite precipitous, but well defined.

About 15 minutes beyond the rock overhang the path turns a corner and starts climbing up the slope. Now you're into Corridor Ravine, and the top is about half an hour away. This is probably one of the gentlest slopes up Table Mountain, but just to balance things out, you'll be going down one of the steepest descents: Woody Ravine!

After a rest at the top, turn left onto the main Twelve Apostles path, and after 5 minutes you should come to the crest of Slangolie Buttress. Keep a sharp lookout for a path off to the left, just 5 m short of the crest. Follow this path for 3 or 4 minutes through waist-high fynbos to a clump of rocks on the right. When the path reaches the rocky outcrop, go straight in through a crack in the rocks marked by a small, stunted Yellowwood Tree. The crack goes some 20 m in and then turns sharp left and over a hump. Suddenly you're into Tranquillity Cracks, a labyrinth of natural corridors with Yellowwoods reaching up to the strip of sky above.

Pristine, tranquil, serene – Tranquillity Cracks is all of these things. Rest here and leave the other world behind for a while ...

Retrace your steps to the main path and turn left towards Table Mountain. Five minutes later you will reach a cliff edge. Either take the easy rock scramble straight down, or the longer way around to the right. Either way you finish up at the top of Slangolie Ravine. Continue up the other side and on the main path for about 5 minutes until you see a weird rock formation on the left eroded by wind and rain over many thousands of years. It's known as the Saucy Dog, because from the northern aspect it resembles a dog sitting up and begging.

Some 25 m beyond the Saucy Dog there is a cairn marking the path down Three Firs Route, which is not recommended as a descent due to erosion. Seven or eight minutes further on you will reach the top of Woody Ravine, clearly marked with a metal sign. The down trip to the Pipe Track is only about 20 – 30 minutes from here – the same time it took you to climb up Corridor Ravine. Although it is very much steeper, the steps are well spaced all the way down. It's like running down the Eiffel Tower, which I was once crazy enough to do. After a rest on the Pipe Track to get rid of the knee wobbles, retrace your steps to your car.

SUIKERBOSSIE CIRCUIT 6

Time: *6 hours*
Grade: *3C*
Water: *Available*

This is another of my favourite walks even though it is more lengthy than it is strenuous. A large portion of it is on the flat, but parts also wind through some magnificent ravines. The ravine you climb up, in particular, is unequalled anywhere on Table Mountain and the Cape Peninsula for its pristine beauty.

The route takes you from near the Suikerbossie Restaurant on the nek between Llandudno and Hout Bay in an easterly direction below Geel-klip Buttress to Myburgh's Waterfall Ravine. This magnificent ravine is deep and narrow and endowed with some huge indigenous trees of which the Knysna Forest would be justly proud. The route goes up the ravine, then across the top, past Judas Peak, and down again via Llandudno Ravine.

There are only a few sections which warrant the 'C' grading: first a steep climb around the actual waterfall in Myburgh's Waterfall Ravine, then the trickiest bit, a climb up a 45- to 60-degree cascade at the top of Myburgh's Waterfall Ravine. I hesitate to call it a waterfall, as it's more of a steep rocky slope down which, in winter anyway, the water cascades. For this reason I would recommend you walk this route in summer when this section is relatively dry. I have done it in winter without too much difficulty, but some people might feel a little uneasy on the wet rocks. Late December to early February are recommended when the Red Disas abound in Myburgh's Waterfall Ravine.

To get to the starting point, turn off the main coastal road between Llandudno and Hout Bay, about 200 m on the Hout Bay side of the top of the hill. Here you will find a signboard to Suikerbossie Restaurant. It was from the Suikerbossie Restaurant parking area that this walk used to begin. However, in August 1990 extensive fencing was erected, effectively cutting off access to the mountain from this convenient starting point. Even worse, the adjoining Ruyterplaats, for centuries a sprawling private estate, has fallen to the property developers, and has likewise been fenced off. However, thanks to sympathetic developers, hikers still have access to the mountain at this point, albeit temporarily.

Suikerbossie Circuit

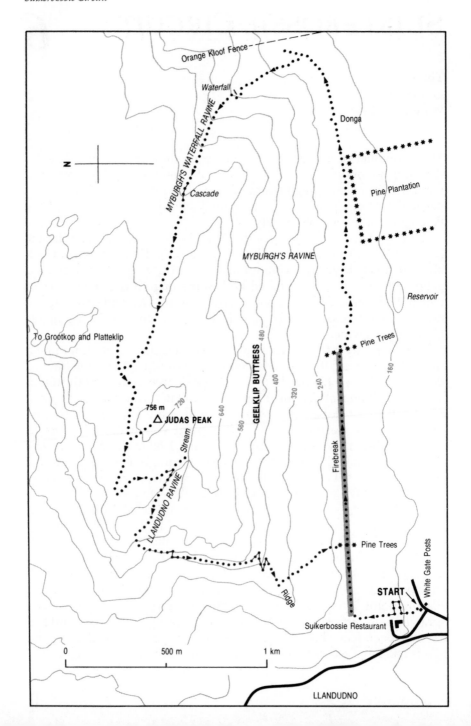

Park your car on the verge, near the white pillars of the Ruyterplaats Estate entrance, some 200 m after the main road turn-off. This access will be available until the end of 1991. After that ask the security guard on the gates where the new access point is.

Walk through the gates and turn half left to go up a path, which 50 m on leads you to some staff cottages, from which you are separated by a fence. Follow this fence around to the right for about 50 m. The fence encloses an underground reservoir, which supplies some of Hout Bay's water. You need to follow the fence around three sides of the reservoir's perimeter. Having completed three sides of the square, continue up the avenue of pines to the wide firebreak near the top of the hill.

Once on the open firebreak, get onto a clear path running down its central spine. It will soon lead you over a rise, and a north-south line of pine trees will come into sight directly ahead. The path passes straight through the pines and continues on towards the next line of pines ahead in the distance. About 200 m after the first line of pines, look up to your left and see Judas Cave at the base of a series of black streaks high up on the buttress above, and don't miss the charming view to the right of Hout Bay nestling between the mountains like a Swiss lake.

As you pass through the second row of pines, the path turns to the right for 10 m before straightening out again. Notice the bad infestation of Stinkbean (wattle). The path is much narrower now, but keep heading in an easterly direction towards a koppie with a remarkable resemblance to Lion's Head. Soon you step over a water pipeline and the path dips down into Myburgh's Ravine (not to be confused with Myburgh's Waterfall Ravine, which is the next one). Cross over Myburgh's Ravine and continue in the same direction for another 15 minutes, after which you will reach a thickly wooded ravine. This is Myburgh's Waterfall Ravine and it is your route up the mountain. It should have taken you about one hour to this point.

Do not follow the path down into the ravine, but rather look for a path going sharply off to the left at the very edge of the indigenous forest. Follow this path up the left bank of the ravine: it gradually becomes fainter and eventually peters out amongst the trees and rocks. Your aim is to climb up the left bank of the ravine for about 15 minutes before coming to the waterfall. At first the path stays high up on the bank and then descends to alongside the stream. Keep to the left bank all the way.

This exceptionally beautiful waterfall was rather spoilt in January 1986 when a 20-m high Rooiels crashed down from above. Since then heavy rains have caused even more trees to come unstuck from the cliffs.

After a rest at the waterfall, follow the base of the cliff face on the Hout Bay side of the waterfall until you come to a point about 30 m further along where it is possible to climb up the steep embankment. The path clings to the steep face of the bank and care should be taken not to dislodge loose rocks. Suddenly you find yourself above the canopy of the forest. When you are almost above the top of the waterfall, keep a sharp eye open for a path diving down to the right. This is the way down to the head of the waterfall. Continuing on the more obvious upward path will only lead you into dense wood.

From here on you need no directions, for you have no alternative but to follow the river bed. You are now in a naturalist's heaven where majestic Yellowwoods reach for the narrow slit of sky and literally hundreds of Red Disas flower in the summer season. Water trickles down off fine moss, like the strings of a harp. It is a very special ravine, reaching back in time to another era when the earth was young and unscathed by civilization. The higher up you go, the narrower it becomes, until you reach a point where the two cliff faces are a mere 5 m apart, yet they reach perhaps 40 to 50 m up.

Shortly after the narrowest section you will come to the base of the second waterfall, or cascade in this case. The easiest way up is straight up the waterfall itself. Stay on the right-hand side, at least for the first half. If there is too much water, there is an alternate route up the steep earth embankment. Five metres beyond the beginning of the rocky cascade, turn sharp right up the embankment. It's very steep and not recommended unless the alternative is too wet. In any event, it joins the cascade again halfway up, but takes you past the wettest parts.

Pause to observe the superb view, over the treetops in Orange Kloof, of the Cape Flats and False Bay through the gap of Constantia Nek.

You will reach a point about three-quarters of the way up the cascade where you need to cross over to the left bank, and here you will find a steep path which will take you to the top, following the general direction of the river.

Once near the top, the path gradually moves away from the river on the left bank. At this point, look around you. On the far right is the huge massif of Grootkop. Ahead is a rocky ridge with what appears to be a cave near its right end. On your left is an unnamed ridge. You should be aiming for the main gap between 'left' ridge and 'cave' ridge. If you haven't found the path at the top left of the cascade, beat around until you find it: it's your ticket home! The path skirts the extreme left-hand side of the valley formed between 'left' ridge and 'cave' ridge. As long as you keep to the left-hand side of the valley, you can't go wrong. The path is hidden in dense bush, but it's clear enough once you're on it. Finding it in the first place is the trick.

About 20 minutes after leaving the top of the cascade you'll start running out of ridge on the left, then suddenly the trig beacon on Judas Peak pops up in front of you on the left. The path then swings right, through a marshy area before it reaches a region of large, flat rocks, level with the ground. Look out for a cairn which marks the point where you join the main north-south 'highway' from the Back Table to Hout Bay: the junction is not very clear because of the rocky surface. At the cairn turn sharp left towards the Judas Peak beacon. The path should soon become clear and you'll pass Judas Peak on your left. The detour to Judas Peak is well worth the view and it will take you about 10 minutes to get there. Remember, you are still $1\frac{1}{2}$ hours from your car. Don't turn off to Judas Peak until the beacon is 45 degrees behind you.

After your detour to this splendid viewpoint (there is a lean-to cave under the beacon on the Hout Bay side), return to the main path which immediately begins to descend towards the sea. Suddenly Sandy Bay and Klein Leeukoppie come into view. Notice, above Klein Leeukoppie, the old army barracks for the radar station near the top of Karbonkel-berg. On the way down the path swings to the left. If uncertain, look for cairns to guide you.

After about 10 minutes of gradual descent in the direction of Hout Bay, the path does a sharp right turn at a cairn perched on a metre-high rock. It almost doubles back on itself. This turn is easily missed and occurs about 100 m before you reach a stream at the foot of the valley. The path carries on to the stream: if you get that far, you will know that you need to retrace your steps. You should not have to start climbing up again, and whatever you do, don't follow the stream down.

The sharp right turn will, within a few hundred metres, bring you to the top of Llandudno Ravine. The northerly descent is steep and narrow. Near the bottom keep right to get to a short 4-m rock scramble. Now the path doubles back on itself and heads in the direction of Hout Bay again, soon to begin a zigzag descent to a lower ridge. At one point you may be tempted to go up, but don't do this.

Note the green gun battery below, just above the coastal road. This forms part of the Apostle Battery, which was officially closed down in December 1943. Its guns were never fired in anger, but it is said that nearly all the windows in Llandudno were broken during its one and only practice shoot.

Cross under a small waterfall (in winter). You are now on a contour path which continues at the same level on a wide bushy ledge for a few hundred metres (about 12 minutes) towards Klein Leeukoppie. Confetti Bush, a type of Buchu, grows on this ledge in great profusion. Take the tiny leaves and crush them between forefinger and thumb: the pleasant smell will linger with you right until your bath. In spring this shrub lives up to its common name when it is covered with tiny white flowers.

At the corner of the mountain you will see a prominent cairn on a rock. On reaching it, look down in the direction of Klein Leeukoppie, and on a lower level you will notice another cairn on a rock. Beyond that a path runs along the top of a ridge. This path is your next destination, and leads you down the slope to the line of pine trees you passed through earlier in the day, thus completing the circuit. Beware, however, not to attempt a straight-line approach to the path on the ridge below. The path first zigzags down to the left, but don't be misled into going too far left. Always come back to the right, remembering your objective. Once down to the line of pines, you should get back to your car in a little over 10 minutes.

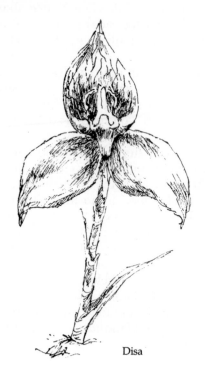

Disa

KAPTEIN'S PEAK 7

Time: $2\frac{1}{2}$ *hours*
Grade: *2B*
Water: *None available*

When I was writing *Twenty Walks Around Hout Bay*, I overlooked this little gem. I had not even bothered to climb it, thinking it was insignificant and too close to civilization. Just how wrong can you be? It offers a charming bird's-eye view of Hout Bay, and on the way an utterly breathcatching 'long drop' a mere 100 m away from a point past which I had walked for years, totally oblivious of this remarkable sight.

Start by driving past Mariner's Wharf at the northern end of Hout Bay Harbour. Take the first major turn right and then turn right again beyond the Sentinel School. Turn right once again beyond the community hall and library and make your way to the top right-hand corner of the housing development. You need to get to the very top end of Bay View Road, where you will find a locked gate closing off a gravel track. Leave your car here, being careful not to block anyone's driveway. This road leads to the old radar station on Karbonkelberg.

Technically you need permission from the SA Navy to use this road, but as you're not going to the radar station, I trust that they won't mind too much. Take a note of the time when you leave your car. After about 15 minutes you'll come to a second gate. Squeeze around to the left of it and start to enjoy the unfolding panorama. Kommetjie Lighthouse has popped out from behind the Sentinel, the broad stretch of Noordhoek Beach flanks Chapman's Bay (the oldest English name on the South African coast), and Hout Bay Harbour lies below, a glistening jewel in the crown of the Fairest Cape.

Just around the second corner beyond the second gate you'll see the radar station on the skyline ahead of you. Built during 1944, it was the first such installation in South Africa and indeed one of only a few in the world. Its height above sea level gave it quite exceptional performance and probably made it unique at the time.

About 30 minutes after leaving your car, the road widens to about three times its normal width and becomes very sandy over a stretch of about 25 m. This is the point at which you leave the road. You will have noticed a clear firebreak on the left, at right angles to the road. (This

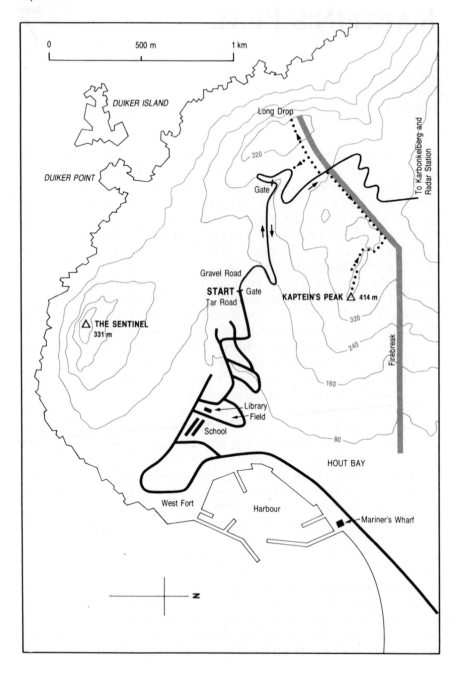

leads to the 'long drop' which we'll visit on the way back.) Its continuation to the right, up the slope through a cutting in the bank, is your way. A 10-minute climb up this firebreak will take you to the crest of the hill. About 50 m before the firebreak starts descending again, look out for a rocky beacon indicating a faint path off to the right. You should now be heading straight towards Kaptein's Peak in an easterly direction. Just before the path comes up against a rocky ridge, bear right and follow the clear path which traverses the Sentinel side of the ridge. Just as it begins to appear impassable, the path does a sharp 90-degree upward left turn into a little gully. Once up the gully and on the crest, turn right towards the Constantiaberg mast, and follow the path winding its way between large boulders.

Shortly before reaching the trig beacon atop Kaptein's Peak you walk into a tranquil milkwood grove with interesting rock overhangs and crags. You need to scramble up the last couple of metres. Surely this is one of the finest views in the Cape Peninsula: to the north lies Judas Peak (the 'pimple'), Grootkop and the back of Table Mountain. If you look carefully, you can see the chimney of the restaurant on top of Table Mountain, just to the right of Grootkop. The slight nick in the flat table is the top of Platteklip Gorge. The whole of the 'Republic' of Hout Bay is spread out before you. To the east lie Constantiaberg and Chapman's Peak Drive, and to the south see how the peak of the Sentinel fits like a jigsaw piece into the sweep of Chapman's Bay and Noordhoek Beach. At your feet lies the picturesque Hout Bay Harbour with its compatible blend of commercial and pleasure craft.

Once you've taken in the scene, rested and uplifted your soul, retrace your steps back to the gravel road (at the point where the firebreak crosses it). For maximum surprise at the 'long drop', don't cross the road at this point. Rather go down the road a few metres to the lower firebreak running parallel to its partner. Follow it, but don't run as it comes to a very sudden end! This staggering drop must be all of 400 m without touching sides. I have no fear of heights, but I caught my breath when I first saw it. Way below can be seen the path around Karbonkelberg (described in *Twenty Walks Around Hout Bay*). Don't be tempted to throw stones from any mountain. There might well be people below.

About halfway back along the firebreak to the road, a path goes off down to the right. Follow it as a pleasant alternative: it will take you back onto the road further down. The easy lope back to your car should complete a pleasant and eventful walk.

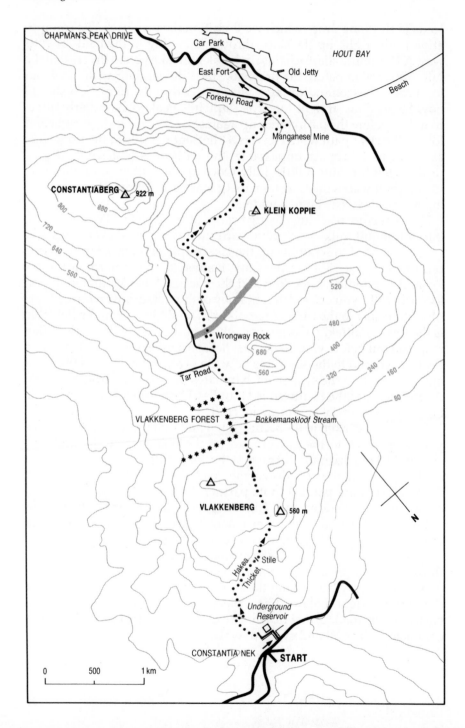

THE MANGANESE MINE   *8*

Time: $4\frac{1}{2}$ *hours*
Grade: 3A
Water: *None available in summer*
Remember to take a torch

This walk is strenuous only as regards its duration and affords some of the most splendid land and sea views in the Peninsula. In addition you can explore a fascinating old mine which penetrates all of 84 m into the mountainside. It is inadvisable to enter the shafts in winter, as they are often wet and slippery.

If you are in a hurry and are prepared to skip the views, you can reach the mine and walk back in about 2 hours, provided you start at the Chapman's Peak Drive end of this walk (*see* map). By far the better alternative, though, is to use two cars. Leave one at the end of the forestry road just beyond East Fort on Chapman's Peak Drive and the other under the trees at Constantia Nek. Walk down from Constantia Nek about 150 m in the direction of Hout Bay until you reach a sign indicating a footpath to Vlakkenberg. Go through the fence at this point and follow the road around the reservoir. Another sign shows the way through the fence at the top left-hand corner of the reservoir area. Now turn left and follow the fence for about 75 m, after which the path veers away and starts to climb first down then up the slope. At the top of the slope it swings sharply to the right after skirting around a fenced off area. The path is very clear, as it has only recently been cut through the dense wattle and hakea infestation. The Long-leafed Wattle (*Acacia longifolia*) on the way up the slope is showing highly encouraging evidence of successful biological control (see page 77).

About half an hour after starting out you will reach a stile and river crossing where there is a notice stating that you need a permit. Don't be too concerned – hordes of hikers use this route every weekend without anybody seeming to bother very much.

Cross over the stream and head for the gap to the left of the beaconed peak high on the skyline. This is Vlakkenberg Nek. You should reach the top within an hour of leaving Constantia Nek.

If you're in this area in spring or summer, once over the nek you'll be amazed at the breathtaking display of wild flowers, particularly the white Everlastings. Now make your way down to the Vlakkenberg Forest, where you need to cross another stream. In winter this stream tends to be a bit slushy, and you may have to cross higher up. Once across, continue on the path up the other side of the valley. After ascending for about 15 minutes, the path suddenly deposits you onto a tarred road – the service road to the Constantiaberg mast.

Follow this road for about 2 minutes to where it turns to the left. At this point leave the road again, following a clear, narrow path to the right (south) which seems to be heading for a point just to the right of the Constantiaberg mast.

Soon the Sentinel comes into view, and along with it a superb view of Hout Bay harbour. You will shortly reach a 2-m high rock next to the path and to the left of it which marks a 4-way intersection. Carry straight on, resisting the temptation to go down to the right. Years ago I was tempted and ended up in impenetrable bush. Ever since, I have known this landmark as 'Wrongway Rock'.

From here it's an easy and pleasant walk, mostly on the level or downhill. Some 15 minutes beyond Wrongway Rock the path takes you into a deep ravine where (in winter) you will find the last source of water on this walk. From the other side of this deep ravine, look back and note the strange rock formation with its vertical rather than horizontal strata. Meantime, below you, Hout Bay continues to present its many varied and beautiful faces.

About 25 minutes later, just before the path descends on a zigzag route down to Chapman's Peak Drive, you'll come across the first of the manganese ore dumps. Continue past them and begin tackling the zigzags down towards the sea. Beyond the fourth bend, and only a few metres before reaching the fifth, a path doubles back. One could almost mistake it for the fifth bend, except that it does not carry on down. Instead it takes you to a gaping hole – No 7 shaft – a couple of hundred metres around the corner in the direction of Hout Bay. Of the eight shafts that make up the Manganese Mine, this has the most impressive entrance by far. It must be all of 15 m high and 3 m wide. However, don't judge this shaft by its entrance: somewhat disappointingly, it penetrates only some 20 m into the mountain. You don't even need a torch.

To reach the deepest shaft (No 4), scramble up to the left of No 7. The shaft you're heading for is about 100 m above and directly in line with No 4. The entrance is large although partly hidden by undergrowth. In the entrance there are three holes, but two of these go straight down to

No 6 shaft below and should be avoided. The third hole is No 4 shaft – at 84 m the longest of them all. You will need a torch to explore it. Even though at the time of writing there were no hidden holes to fall into in the dark, you do enter at your own risk. Considering the primitive tools available in 1909, when the shaft was sunk, it is quite a remarkable feat of tunnelling.

As the manganese was found rather high up on the mountain, an economical means of transporting the ore down to the waiting ships below had to be devised. To get the ore down to the jetty below, the remains of which can still be clearly seen, a chute of corrugated iron was built. This primitive and often rather ineffective construction was over 750 m in length and must have been quite impressive. However, all didn't go as the designers would have liked, because the steep gradient often caused the ore to go out of control.

A popular Hout Bay legend has it that the first load of ore went careering down the chute and straight through the bottom of the waiting ship. Alas, while colourful and amusing, it is simply not true. An examination of the angle of the jetty and its construction shows up the story for what it is – a local myth. Early photographs show that the ore was transported along the jetty in cocopans, quite apart from which there is the notable absence of a wreck to substantiate the tale.

The manganese content of the ore varied greatly. In some cases the iron content (which occurs together with manganese) made a mockery of any reference to a manganese mine. One assay in the largest shaft revealed ore with 43 per cent iron and no manganese at all. A combination of transport problems and the decreasing grade of ore caused the mine to close down in 1911, after only two year's operation.

Find your way back to the zigzag path by which you came down. It will soon lead you to the gravel forestry road below, and to your waiting car parked on Chapman's Peak Drive.

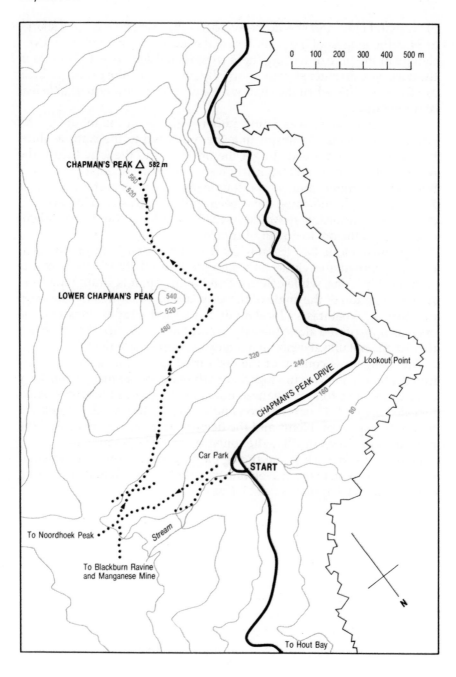

CHAPMAN'S PEAK   *9*

Time: $2\frac{1}{2}$ *hours*
Grade: *2A*
Water: *Available on lower slopes only*

This walk is much easier than it looks. To reach the top requires less than an hour and a half, and the path takes you through some dense stands of proteas whilst presenting you with some breathtaking views. The rocks on top of Chapman's Peak afford protection from the wind and make this an ideal spot to enjoy a late breakfast.

Leave your car at the last big bend before reaching the top of Chapman's Peak Drive, 750 m on the Hout Bay side of the lookout spot.

Log steps lead up from the left-hand side of the picnic area, and just three minutes later cross over the stream. Beyond the stream you are immediately confronted with a fork: do not turn left and follow the river's course, as this path peters out higher up (*see* map). Rather take the right-hand fork and go straight up the slope for 25 m before turning left at a clear T-junction. This path will take you straight up the side of the ravine for another 20 minutes before depositing you on to a flat plateau at the top.

Here you will reach a parting of the ways (*see* map) and a good place for a rest. You need to turn sharp right, in the direction of Chapman's Peak. The path crosses over a firebreak path and then dives into dense stands of proteas on the way to your destination, which is still almost an hour distant. In the early morning or late afternoon you may be treated to delightful song as birds of all descriptions tell of their pleasure in this forest of proteas – mainly Blackbearded Protea, which flowers in winter, and a smattering of Yellow Pincushions.

The path takes you around and to the right of the first peak. Now you can see round the corner of the Sentinel and view the wild Karbonkelberg coastline. Then, suddenly, Chapman's Peak pops up in front of you and Hout Bay slips from view as the path makes its way down through more proteas, across the saddle between 'Lower' Chapman's Peak and Chapman's Peak itself.

As you climb from the saddle to make the final assault, Fish Hoek unexpectedly appears on your left. Now it is an easy scramble to the survey beacon at the top, and the panorama which unfolds from here is well worth all the effort. Not only can you see Hout Bay nestling peacefully below you, but Gordon's Bay in the far distance as well!

Allow 45 minutes to get back to your car on Chapman's Peak Drive (originally known as the 'Hout Bay – Noorde Hoek Road'). Contrary to popular belief it was not built by Italian prisoners-of-war. This would have been rather awkward, as Italy fought on the side of the Allies during World War I, the period during which it was built. (The confusion probably arises from the use made of 5 000 Italian POW's to make a start with the construction of Du Toit's Kloof Pass between 1943 and 1945 during World War II.)

Chapman's Peak Drive was built with the help of convict labour, of which some 700 in all were provided by the newly formed Union Government. Construction started in 1915 from the Hout Bay end, and more than a year later also from the Noordhoek end. In September 1919 the relatively easy stretch from Hout Bay to the lookout was completed, but it was more than 2 years before the Noordhoek stretch caught up. The great day arrived on 6 May 1922, when this magnificent scenic drive was opened by the Governor-General, Prince Arthur of Connaught.

According to the *Cape Times* of Monday 8 May 1922, 'Amongst those present were the Administrator of the Cape, Sir Frederic de Waal, the Archbishop of Cape Town, Dr Carter, Colonel Metz, Colonel Reitz and many members of Parliament, as well as a large number of ladies.' The news reporter makes it sound as though the ladies had been let out for the day!

Prince Arthur drove through a silk ribbon followed by '160 to 170 motor cars and charabancs conveying the invited guests' who were later 'regaled with refreshments'.

Sir Frederic de Waal (who was the main driving force behind this scenic drive and after whom De Waal Drive is named) predicted, 'The day will come when people will get tired of Egypt and other parts of the world and they will come to South Africa to spend two or three months here, when there is winter in England.'

Alas, that day has come and gone. The pace of life is such today that long colonial winter sojourns are very much a thing of the past.

LONG BEACH AND A SHIPWRECK

10

Time: *2 hours*
Grade: *1A*
Water: *None available*

This is a walk for the entire family, including the dog. Along the beach between Kommetjie and Noordhoek you'll be accompanied by the call of gulls and the crash of the waves. The highlight of this walk, apart from the fact that it is totally different from a mountain walk, is a fascinating shipwreck. Depending on which option you choose, this is encountered either at the midpoint or at the end of the walk. The wreck of the *Kakapo* is in fact the midpoint between Kommetjie and Noord-hoek, so you can do one of two things: either walk from Kommetjie to the wreck and return the same way, or go the whole hog and walk the roughly 6 km or so to Noordhoek. However, unless you want to walk all the way back again, this latter option requires that a car be left at the end, which is a time-consuming business in itself.

From Kommetjie (or Noordhoek) to the wreck is about 45 minutes' walk. Give yourself half an hour at the wreck for exploring and refreshments, plus 45 minutes back, which totals 2 hours. It would still be 2 hours if you continued to the other end, but then allow an extra 45 minutes for shunting cars back and forth.

If you're going to walk the full length of the beach, or for that matter the 'half return', then I suggest you start at Kommetjie and not Noord-hoek. There are three reasons for this: The view walking north is far more interesting and if the inevitable south-easter is blowing, rather let it push you, than struggle against it. Lastly, the beach is more interesting and varied at the Kommetjie end. A further word of advice is to choose low tide for your walk, as the going is much easier on the firm sand of the intertidal zone.

Start by driving to the quaint little village of Kommetjie. The name Kommetjie refers to the 'little basin' formed in the rocks of the shoreline which is surrounded by many splendid Milkwoods. Once you reach the outskirts, take the third turn to the right into Kirsten Avenue, and follow the signs to Long Beach, where you will find a parking area adjacent to

Long Beach and a Shipwreck

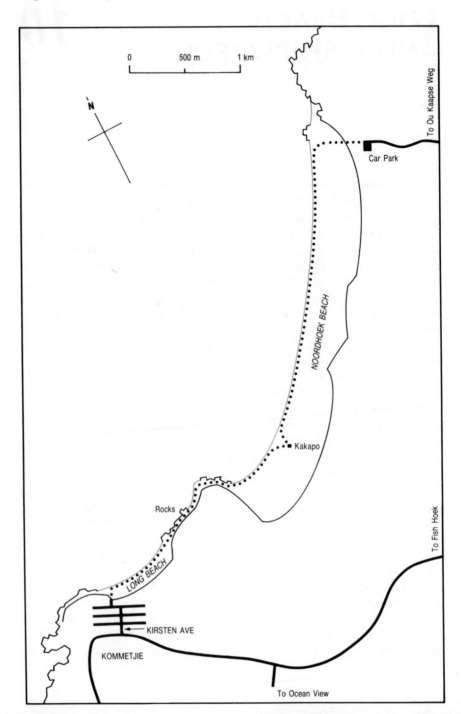

the beach. Leave your car here and walk down to the water's edge: Noordhoek looks a long way off. Soon after you start your walk, you wouldn't be blamed for thinking you were at Arniston, with its quaint thatched and whitewashed beach cottages. The architectural style is so 'Cape Beach' that it almost begs to adorn a calendar.

Ahead you will see the glorious sweep of Hout Bay, from Karbonkelberg on the left (the little pimple on top is the old World War II radar station) through the Sentinel, Klein Leeukoppie, Judas Peak, Grootkop and the flat table top of Table Mountain as seen from behind to Chapman's Peak in the foreground. Provided you have the necessary permit, the rocks on your left are home to tasty black mussels just waiting to be plucked at low tide. Once you get around the rocky corner, about 25 minutes after starting, you'll get a glimpse of the wreck of the *Kakapo*, set back about 100 m above the high-water mark. It will first be seen as a black cylinder with a 'pole' sticking up to the right. The 'cylinder' is the ship's boiler and the 'pole' is the rudder post.

Forty to forty-five minutes from the start and you're there. Notice how the rudder is still in the 'hard-a-port' position, as a lasting reminder of the moment nearly a century ago when the captain desperately tried to correct his unfortunate error. This steamship came ashore under circumstances that were most embarrassing for its master. The vessel was on its way from Table Bay to New Zealand one foul and stormy night in May 1900 whilst on its maiden voyage. As there was no Kommetjie lighthouse in those days (this was built about 1913), the

Wreck of the Kakapo

61

captain mistook Chapman's Peak for Cape Point and did a sharp left turn. With engines at full ahead and the assistance of a gale force following wind and high spring tide, the ship was driven so high and dry onto the beach that the crew were able to walk off at low tide without getting their feet wet. Try explaining that to the shipowners and cargo underwriters back in London!

The ribs of the vessel still stick defiantly out of the sand and give an indication of the *Kakapo's* size. Some of the plates forming the sides of the vessel were removed at one time and were used to prevent sand from blowing over the railway line at Fish Hoek. The boiler is quite fascinating. The three large holes at beach level are the furnaces into which the coal was shovelled: two of them are still exposed enough to climb into. It's not often you can claim to have had tea in the furnace of a ship's boiler! It was a fire-tube boiler and the fire tubes, long since corroded away, connected the battery of holes you see.

Have you ever wondered where a steamship at sea for a month or two got fresh water to feed its boilers, not to mention the crew? I suspect the upright cylindrical structure to the forward starboard side of the boiler is the remains of the ship's evaporator. This used to boil and distil seawater to produce fresh water.

Your walk back to Kommetjie, or on to Noordhoek, will take you about 45 minutes. If you choose to continue to Noordhoek, leave the beach from a point almost directly below the tip of Chapman's Peak. Another car should be waiting for you at the Noordhoek Beach parking area. On your return to Kommetjie, remember that the local hotel serves an excellent crayfish in season at a very reasonable price.

ELSIE'S PEAK *11*

Time: *2 hours*
Grade: *1A*
Water: *None available*

This is a short, easy hike with pleasant views and includes a wonderful example of fynbos triumphing over alien invaders. Drive to Fish Hoek or take the train and make your way to the 3-way traffic circle at the end of Fish Hoek's Main Road. Turn right towards Kommetjie and immediately on your left, just before a church, you'll see a large off-road parking area. Leave your car here and make your way up some public steps named 'Ravine Steps' leading off the left-hand corner of the parking area. These will take you to the top line of houses, where a path continues the upward climb as an extension of the steps. Cross over a firebreak and soon you will come to a T-junction where there is an old sign announcing that you are about to enter the Fish Hoek Municipality Mountain Reserve. Bear half right here. The path traverses to the right, and about 100 m further along doubles back on itself to a higher level.

Up to this point you are still surrounded by alien shrub, but this soon gives way to a superb variety of fynbos, which is a credit to the Fish Hoek Municipality and volunteer conservation groups who have laboriously hacked back the invading Port Jackson and Rooikrans and allowed the indigenous fynbos to re-establish itself, all in the last ten years. As you reach a higher level, look back to your right and see the clearly marked battlefront, indicated by a huge green wall of wattle.

Keep to the left at a faint fork, and some 35 minutes after leaving your car you will arrive at the back of a quarry, which can be clearly seen from Fish Hoek as a pile of stones high on the mountainside. You will recognise it from the loose scree on your left. Just before and just after this point you need to keep your eyes open for forks in the path. Keep left all the way up. The idea is to go up the left-hand fork and return via the right-hand route after visiting the summit.

Some 8 minutes after taking the left-hand fork you'll come to a 2,5-m high rock pinnacle at the edge of the path. Bear right here just before you find yourself between two koppies. The path then climbs up and behind the koppie on the right. About 25 minutes after taking the left-hand fork, you'll find that the other path joins yours again from the

Elsie's Peak

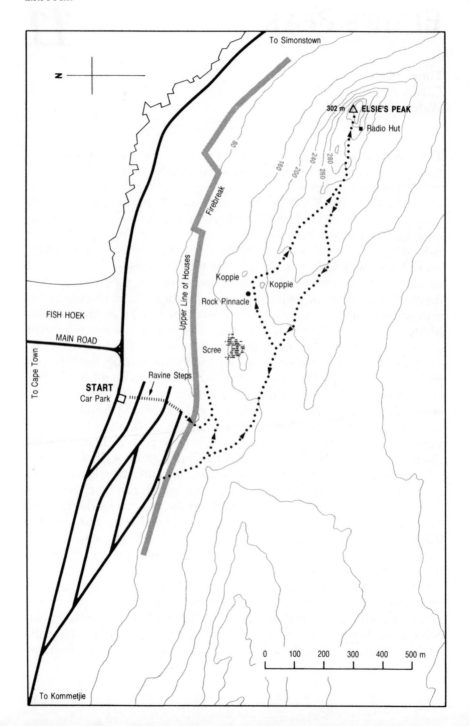

right. Soon you'll see the beacon on Elsie's Peak and the Simon's Town Naval Base will ease into view, nestling peacefully in the lee of the mountain. A peppering of small craft completes the picture.

You pass a radio hut just before you reach Elsie's Peak about one hour after starting. Glencairn is immediately below you on one side, while on the other side Fish Hoek, Kalk Bay and Muizenberg lie at the beginning of a majestic sweep all the way around False Bay to Hangklip. From this point you can clearly see two oceans, as the Atlantic peeps through Noordhoek valley. While looking in that direction, notice the hump in the middle of the Fish Hoek valley on which Peer's Cave is situated. This is the site of many remnants of early man. Should you be up Elsie's Peak in late September or early October, you may be lucky enough to see Southern Right Whales with their calves in False Bay. These whales return year after year to the bay during spring, and although their numbers were reduced rapidly in the past, it is encouraging to see that they are slowly increasing again. A large whaling station was built at Kalk Bay in 1806 but was forced to close five years later because the whale population had declined so dramatically.

It will take you about 30 minutes to get back to the parking area. Remember to go left at the fork 5 minutes after leaving the top to give your return some variety.

Yellow Pincushion

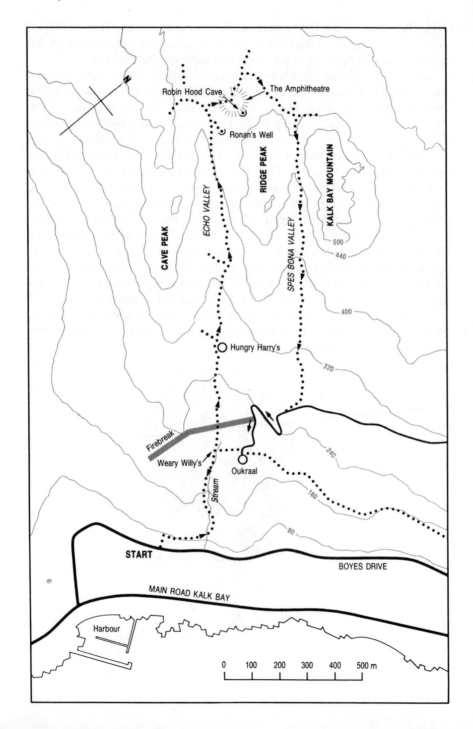

THE AMPHITHEATRE   *12*

Time: *3 hours (allow extra time if you wish to explore the caves)*
Grade: *2A*
Water: *Available*
Remember to bring along a torch

Two delightful indigenous forests and a number of interesting caves are features of this walk.

I was amazed that an old friend of mine who has lived in Cape Town most of his life and is a keen hiker, wasn't aware that the mountains above Kalk Bay and Muizenberg are riddled with caves. In fact there are 67 in all, with names ranging from Devil's Pit to Musical Drops Cave, not to mention such interesting-sounding appellations as Aladdin's Cave, Surprise Grotto, Commemoration Hall and Spookgrot. With as many as 67 caves to choose from, I shall resist the temptation to turn this and the next chapter into a detailed description of them. If you are interested in more than just hiking, then get hold of the detailed guide to the Kalk Bay and Muizenberg caves from the Parks and Forest Branch of the Cape Town City Council.

Begin your hike from Boyes Drive up some steep steps marked by a Silvermine Reserve signpost. The steps are directly opposite and in line with the Kalk Bay Harbour entrance. At the top of the short flight of steps turn right and climb steadily towards Muizenberg. As you ascend the well-worn path, you might hear the clickety-clack of a passing train, or look down onto the picturesque fishing harbour while stopping for a rest. Kalk Bay got its name from the days of Simon van der Stel when kilns were used to burn seashells to produce lime (kalk) for mortar for buildings throughout the Peninsula. The limestone origins of the caves might also have had some say in the matter.

A few hundred metres on, the path turns sharp left up the mountain, up some well-placed stone steps and over a few wooden foot bridges. About 20 to 25 minutes after starting, you will arrive at Weary Willy's, a small clearing with a 'sitting stone' in the middle of it. Your return route brings you back to this point from across the stream on your right. Continue the path upward, heading for a large clump of rocks ahead of you at the base of Echo Valley, which is bounded on the left by Cave Peak and on the right by Ridge Peak. The large clump of rocks should be reached about 35 to 40 minutes after starting and is known as Hungry Harry's Halfway Halt. It is indeed about halfway between the start and your tea stop and terminus, The Amphitheatre. Hungry Harry's, also known as Cavern Rocks, is a good spot for a rest, as it provides shelter from all kinds of weather.

A mere 15 m beyond the short turn-off to Hungry Harry's a path breaks off to the left. Do not take it. Merely note, for a future adventure, that it goes to the south face of Cave Peak, which is rich in interesting caves, in particular Boomslang Cave, which penetrates 150 m right through the mountain. Your way is straight on and up Echo Valley. A few minutes later you'll see another path breaking off to the left. This comes down from the northern exit of Boomslang Cave after it has gone through Cave Peak. This cave, one of the finest on the mountain, is not recommended in winter as it is too wet.

Look back and see Hangklip framed between Ridge and Cave peaks. This is a good growing area for South Africa's national flower, the King Protea (*Protea cynaroides*). Soon the path dives into a magnificent Yellowwood and Milkwood grove which must surely bring back childhood memories of Walt Disney's Magic Forest. You almost expect to see Bambi, Snow White and other characters frolicking here. You emerge from the magic forest all too soon at the head of the valley.

Two minutes after emerging from the dense forest, as the path climbs up the right slope for a short distance, another path turns off the main one sharply to the right. Take this slight detour upwards for 10 m and another 10 m to the right to bring you to the opening of Ronan's Well. This is not a cave for amateurs, but is interesting to look into, and it always has water. The entrance to the cave proper is near the ceiling at the far end of the cavern.

At the ripe old age of 14, I was convinced that my days had come to an end when I got stuck in this cave, well beyond what was then the official limit! Since then it has been opened up and at 400 m is the longest cave in these mountains. It is also one of the most dangerous, so don't even think about exploring it!

Return to the main path. A few minutes later the path forks. Take the right-hand fork, which will lead you into The Amphitheatre within a couple of minutes. The Amphitheatre can best be described as a box canyon. It's an ideal spot for a rest. In the far right-hand corner a clump of trees hides Robin Hood Cave (also not recommended for beginners).

After resting and refreshing yourself, your way out is up the far left-hand corner as seen from the point where you came in. This path

King Protea

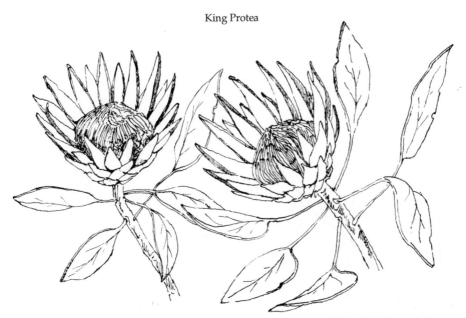

takes you past a few other caves in the area and finally forks 25 m short of the top of the ridge. Take the right-hand fork in the direction of a very weathered rock on the horizon. Once past the rock, head back towards False Bay. Suddenly Simon's Town Naval Base pops into view.

The white trig beacon you see is atop Kalk Bay Mountain. Keep heading in its general direction. Shortly after it disappears from view, you will come to a four-way junction. Turn right towards Spes Bona, and on reaching the crest of the valley descend into another lovely indigenous forest, this time mainly Yellowwoods. In some places they are so intertwined with Milkwoods that different leaves seem to be growing on the same tree. Nature has painted the rocks green with moss and the trees assume the most contorted shapes: nothing seems to grow straight up in this fascinating forest.

Five minutes after emerging from the Spes Bona forest, you will see a gravel road below you. On reaching the road, head towards Simon's Town, following the winding gravel road down for about 500 m to where it narrows to a broad path at a green City Council rubbish bin: this is Oukraal. Now take the path straight down into the kloof and back to Weary Willy's, from where you retrace your steps to Boyes Drive.

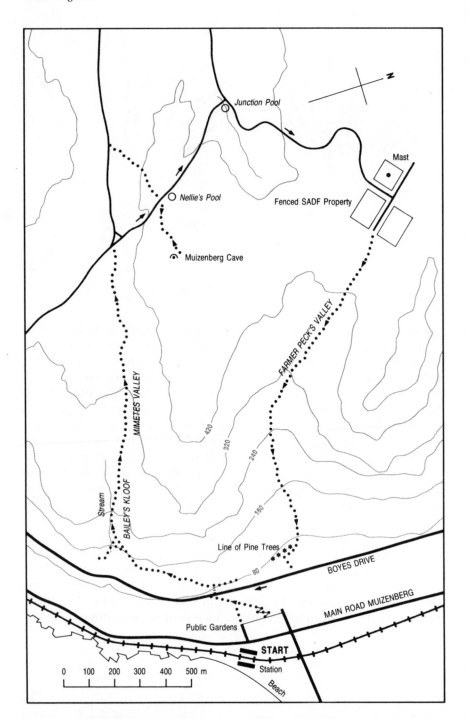

MUIZENBERG CAVE 13

Time: *3 hours*
Grade: *2A*
Water: *Available*
Remember to bring a torch

Where else in the world can you get on a train, travel a relatively short distance (in this case to Muizenberg), and get off at a station where the sea and a length of beautiful beach stretch far into the distance from one platform – and towering above the other platform is a mountain which takes little more than an hour to climb to the top. Just to add to all this, history surrounds you, and the views, as well as the plant and bird life en route, are magnificent.

Even if you haven't travelled on a train for years, why not take a trip to Muizenberg this weekend, and do a circular hike around the mountain above Muizenberg station? It's called St James' Peak. (Just to confuse you, Muizenberg Peak is the one above False Bay station, and your destination, Muizenberg Cave, is on St James' Peak. Work that one out if you can.)

Start from Muizenberg station and turn right towards the very pleasant public gardens on the slopes below Boyes Drive. School Road runs up the left-hand side of the public gardens to the police station at the top. Once at the top of School Road, keep going up across a short stretch of grass until you reach a gravel path that runs from right to left. Walk up this path until you finally reach Boyes Drive above. Almost directly opposite, but perhaps some 15 m to the right, some crude steps go straight up the mountain. You should by now be opposite the clock tower on the station.

After leaving Boyes Drive, some 3 minutes of uphill slog will bring you to a T-junction where you should turn left towards Simon's Town. Ten minutes further on you'll reach a fork. Keep right for 3 minutes until you come to a barbed wire reclamation fence to the left of the path. Opposite the fence some steep steps ascend sharply to the right. Take these steps, and you're on your way up Bailey's Kloof. Look down and see Bailey's Cottage, a thatched-roof abode almost in the sea. It once belonged to Abe Bailey (1865 – 1940), a man who featured prominently as a mining magnate and politician around the turn of the century. It is

71

at this very spot that the Battle of Muizenberg took place nearly two centuries ago. It's hard to imagine that this peaceful little corner of False Bay could have been the scene of such conflict. Picture eighteen English warships with sails set like bulging chests pounding the Dutch troops on the shore. The Dutch fell back and dug in at a place now called Retreat! This battle was of no small significance, for it changed 150 years of Dutch occupation to 150 years of British domination.

However, history is not the only thing of interest on this easy hike around the mountain. Flowering during spring from August to December is an uncommon species of Erica called *Erica urna-viridis* (the Latin name meaning 'resembling a green urn'). It's a very pretty, almost white-greenish Erica, sticky to the touch. What is so special about it is that it occurs only on this mountain above Muizenberg and nowhere else in the world. On one occasion I saw this extremely rare plant in three separate locations, and I wasn't even looking for it.

But let us tear ourselves away from history and botanical rarities, and continue the slog up Bailey's Kloof. Rest occasionally on the steep stone steps (which in themselves represent a labour of love) to see the full sweep of False Bay from Hangklip to Cape Point. After some ten minutes up these steep steps, you meet various paths. Just remember you need to go up, and straight, along the gently sloping valley which begins to open up before you. This is where Bailey's Kloof leads into Mimetes Valley. Keep straight ahead and just to the right of and parallel to a small stream. A short wire fence spanning the stream shows the way. Mimetes Valley is named after a member of the Protea family, *Mimetes fimbriifolius*, a stout, dense shrub or small tree which flowers between June and November in a brilliant splash of red.

The path veers gently away from the stream to the right-hand side of the valley. After about half an hour of easy walking up Mimetes Valley (pronounced My Meetees) from the top of Bailey's Kloof the path spills out onto a gravel road, which immediately presents you with three possibilities. Take the right-hand fork up. After 200 m, keep a sharp eye open for a path off the gravel road to the right, turning half back. Five minutes' walk up this path will bring you to Muizenberg Cave, to the right of the path at the top of the ridge.

Within the large, gaping entrance to the cave, there are two smaller entrances on the right-hand side of the main chamber. Take the first and larger of these, provided you have a torch. This leads, within a few metres, to a 6-m deep well. Care should be taken here, as the rocks can be slippery. At the well, turn sharp left and walk for another few metres until you come to a T-junction. A left turn will lead you back to the main entrance chamber. A right turn will take you 40 m through the mountain on hands and knees to emerge on the southern side of the ridge.

Leave the cave the same way you came up and return to the gravel road. On reaching it, turn right and continue up the slope. Within a few metres you will pass Nellie's Pool on the right. The gravel road takes you over the rise and downhill to Junction Pool. On the way down, notice the Ou Kaapse Weg in the distance as a reminder that civilization isn't far away. Junction Pool is a pleasant grassy picnic spot where there's always water. Cross the river and at the T-junction turn right. Now follow this road through fields of indigenous Geelbos which at times of the year are such a brilliant yellow as to be almost loud!

Some 15 minutes beyond Junction Pool the road runs alongside the fence guarding an SA Defence Force mast. (The vertical wires of varying lengths are the aerials, and not the mast structure itself.) On the far side of the mast area the road forks to the right and 3 or 4 minutes later you reach a corridor between two more fenced-off areas, after which the gravel road stops abruptly and becomes a track. You are now at the top of Peck's Valley, named after the brothers Peck who ran the well-known and popular Farmer Peck's Inn, which in the early to mid-1800s stood on the site now occupied by a tall block of flats.

Suddenly Muizenberg Corner pops into view. Notice the quaint and colourful bathing boxes so well known from postcards and calendars: a legacy from a by-gone era. If you thought the steps on the way up were a labour of love, what about these down Peck's Valley? A great deal of sweat and toil must have gone into making your journey down a more comfortable one.

Near the bottom of the valley the path veers to the right. Halfway along a line of pine trees and opposite an old ruin, take the steps down to Boyes Drive. Some 150 m along Boyes Drive to the south you should find the path on which you came up from the station.

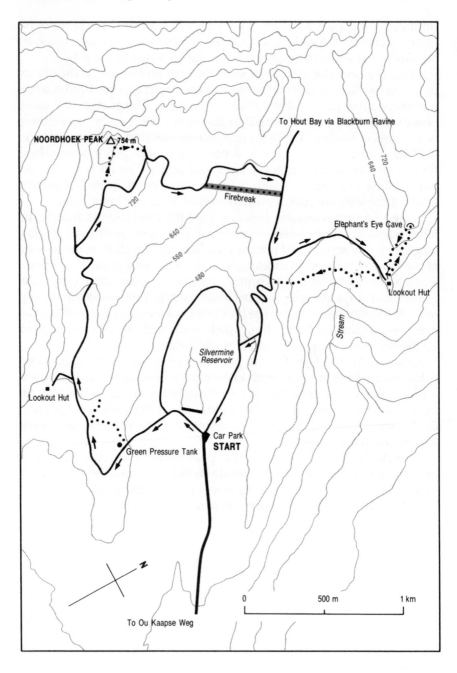

SILVERMINE CIRCUIT AND ELEPHANT'S EYE CAVE

14

Time: *3 hours; allow 1 hour extra to get to and explore the cave*
Grade: *2A*
Water: *Available only at the beginning and the end*

This walk is almost entirely along gravel roads, which makes it easy going. There are two glorious viewpoints en route.

The name Silvermine is a complete misnomer; although shafts were sunk in the area between 1675 and 1685, not one ounce of silver was discovered. Drive to the top of Ou Kaapse Weg from the direction of Cape Town and turn right into the western half of the Silvermine Nature Reserve. You'll be required to pay a modest fee at the gate, immediately beyond which you have a choice of taking a left turn or going straight ahead. Follow the tarred road straight ahead for 2,4 km until you reach a parking area just to the right of the Silvermine Reservoir wall.

Leave your car here, note the time and take the gravel track which cuts across the valley below the reservoir wall. Once you've reached the end of the wall, bear left, following the gravel road on its gentle ascent. The reservoir was built in 1898 by the old Kalk Bay Municipality to supply water for its residents, but is now used solely for the purpose of watering the Westlake golf course. When the reservoir is full and the surrounding pines are reflected in the quiet waters, one is instantly reminded of a tranquil Canadian lake. Keep to the main road and ignore the side roads to left and right. However, you might wish to take a short cut to the right marked 'Noordhoek Peak', next to a green 2-m high cylindrical pressure tank. If you take this option, be sure to turn left at the T-junction near the top of the ridge, to get back onto the gravel road. It's perhaps safer to stick to the road, being easier and only about 100 m longer. Assuming you stay on the road, it soon sweeps round a sharp right-hand curve and the Noordhoek lookout hut comes into view. What appears to be a fork in the road further on is merely a side track to this hut. The 3-minute detour is worth it just for the view: Fish Hoek, Simon's Town and Noordhoek look great from here.

From the fork, the road climbs steadily for some way before negotiating three sharp bends. Soon after the third bend you'll reach another fork, with a sandy track off to the left. Ignore it and keep half right along the gravel. At this point, however, there is a short 10-m path sharp left to another viewpoint over Noordhoek. Approximately 6 to 8 minutes further on, you will come to a fairly substantial stone pillar built to the left of the road. It proudly announces 'Footpath', and at first glance it seems such a grandiose sign for such an insignificant pathway. However, when you see the view to which it leads you, the pillar seems quite inadequate, for this path is a must: it leads you to a stone pyramid a few hundred metres up ahead which marks Noordhoek Peak. It has probably taken you about an hour to reach the peak.

Surely this is the most photogenic view in all of the Western Cape? A matter of opinion obviously, but on a clear day it is quite superb. For the best photographs make sure you get there by late morning, otherwise you'll be looking into the sun.

On leaving Noordhoek Peak, don't retrace your steps, but rather fork to the left, which will lead you back to the gravel road further down. The road now descends gently for about half an hour before sweeping to the right, into the home stretch. At this point another road joins in from the left and behind, coming from the top of Blackburn Ravine above Hout Bay. This is the 'Old Road to Hout Bay', and you are on it. It went from the Tokai forest, along this road and down Blackburn Ravine into Hout Bay. It could only have been used by pack mules and horses, as I can't imagine oxwagons making their way down the steep slopes of Blackburn Ravine.

After walking along the 'Old Road' for about 8 minutes, you'll come to a T-junction, just before the road dips down and is reinforced with a double concrete strip. A metal pole marks the T-junction: presumably it was a signpost pointing the way to Elephant's Eye Cave. At this point you need to decide whether or not you have time to divert to Elephant's Eye Cave. It's situated just around the corner from the Lookout Hut you can see on the ridge. It will take you 15 minutes to reach the hut and a further 10 minutes to the cave, so allow an hour for the diversion.

Once at the Lookout Hut, you can't miss the cave, as it's a gaping black hole in the cliff face. From most parts of Tokai this bit of mountain takes on the shape of an elephant's head, with the cave in just the right place for an eye. From this substantial cave you have a sweeping view of False Bay all the way to Hangklip. Pick out the Rondevlei bird sanctuary as well as Zeekoevlei, Sandvlei and Marina da Gama.

Silvermine Reservoir

You can get back to the Lookout Hut and the Old Road via an alternative and more interesting route. Leave the cave at the highest level possible against the rock face, traverse above the point where you came up, then climb down some log steps. Once on the road, cross over it, aiming for the white sandy path skirting the right-hand edge of the pine forest below, then cross over the river (the only source of water on this hike). On the left, after crossing the river, you might notice the results of some fascinating biological control. Long-leaf wattle (*Acacia longifolia*) appear to be covered in large green and brown berries. These 'berries' are in fact the result of a wasp (imported from Australia, like the wattle itself) that lays its eggs in the ovary of the flower. The flower aborts, and grows a wart-like growth around the invaders. If you were to take a penknife and carefully cut one of these in half, you'll find two or three wriggling grubs inside, but only if the berry is green. If it's brown, look for the minute holes on the outside where the grubs burrowed their way out to repeat the cycle. Perhaps this kind of biological control is the only way in which we will be able to eradicate this serious alien invasion.

Once back on the gravel road you zigzag down to the level of the reservoir. Don't be tempted to cut corners and add to soil erosion. You need to get to the darker of the two parallel roads you see below you (the one nearer the dam). It will lead you straight back to your car. This is a popular braai spot during summer. With proper planning you could even arrange to have some hot coals and a cold beer waiting for you!

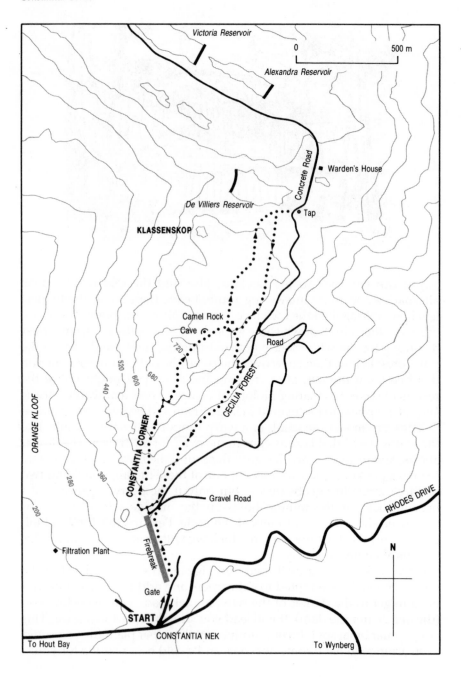

CONSTANTIA CORNER 15

Time: $3\frac{1}{2}$ *hours*
Grade: *3C*
Water: *None available*

This is another of my favourite walks. It is relatively short, fairly strenuous and offers magnificent alternating views of Orange Kloof and the Cape Flats. An added bonus is that you'll be in shade for most of the way up, provided you start by 09h00.

Leave your car in the parking area on the north side of Constantia Nek. Take the narrow tarred road leading up alongside some houses (not the one leading into Orange Kloof). Three minutes up this road, you'll come to a locked gate across the road. You have just walked up the last remaining section of the original Rhodes Drive, which was built for Cecil Rhodes to travel through his vast estate. Go around the gate, and about 25 m beyond it, on the edge of a pine forest, you'll find some steps marked 'Back Table' ascending to the left. The well-cut log steps take you up a steady climb more or less along the edge of the forest. Some quarter of an hour later they'll deliver you onto a gravel road. At the gravel road, turn left and follow it to its end, a mere 100 m away. At the end of the road, take the footpath going up to the right. This will take you 50 m up to a cliff face, where it turns sharp left. On the way up to the cliff face you'll be tempted by a few left turns which do not matter as they all end up at the same spot anyway. It's just easier to go right up to the cliff face.

Traverse around to above Orange Kloof and Hout Bay on a clear path through what were once dense stands of Protea bushes, devastated by fire in February 1990. If in doubt, keep right. Eventually it will lead you into a ravine about 35 to 40 minutes after leaving your car. At this point turn upwards into the ravine. A rocky cairn will show you the point where you should turn upwards. Keep to the right-hand side of the ravine and avoid the scree in the middle.

You will soon be on the ridge known as Constantia Corner, which separates Cecilia Forest and Orange Kloof (the one planted by man and the other by nature). The path then zigzags up this ridge, giving you wonderful alternating views of Constantia and Hout Bay. Shortly you'll zigzag back into the top part of the ravine you started up. The path should always be perfectly clear and well defined: if not, retrace your steps. Sometimes on the zigzag you'll be faced with a choice of two clear paths. Take either, as they soon join again.

At the top of the ravine the path eases to a gentle slope, taking you to the base of a cliff face. You should have reached this point more or less an hour after starting. Look down over the burgeoning, but still beautiful, Hout Bay Valley. I have lived there since 1970, and still find it as enchanting as ever. Don't let the cliff face intimidate you as the path finds an easy scrambling route up it. Only those with a severe fear of heights might experience some difficulty. Soon a trig beacon comes into sight, followed by a flat stretch of about 100 m which leads to another cliff barrier. This time the path leads you through a gap in the cliff, over and down into a superb spot for a rest. Here two huge rock overhangs form a welcome stop and provide shelter from the wind and the weather, be it hot or cold.

When rested, cross the valley floor in front of the 'cave' and look up to see Camel Rock, one of many bizarre weather-beaten rocks in this little valley. It doesn't have much of a hump, but its neck is certainly better defined than the one at Scarborough. It is an important landmark, because here you have a choice of paths at the bottom of the valley it overlooks.

Turn right if you're in a hurry. This is a shortcut, and as long as you keep going right, it will eventually bring you back to where you started. Your second choice is to carry on up to the base of Camel Rock and on to the Back Table. This route is only an extra 25 minutes walking time, and is well worth the trouble.

From Camel Rock the path continues north for 5 minutes until the forester's cottage and concrete road pop into sight. At the last moment the De Villiers Reservoir comes into view. This is the southernmost of the five reservoirs on the Back Table. About 50 m before reaching the concrete road, you're faced with another decision. If you want to take the easy but less interesting way down to Constantia Nek via the road, do just that. If, on the other hand, you want to try a path which skirts above the road and is much more pleasant but somewhat precipitous in places, then look for the right-hand turn back up the koppie about 50 m before reaching the road. It is a clear path, almost a firebreak, and does not peter out. This path affords superb views of False Bay and the southern Peninsula which you will miss on the concrete road as it winds through dense pine plantations.

After 10 minutes along the upper path you'll meet the path coming down from Camel Rock. Continue along it down to lower levels. From here the path plunges steeply down and crosses the end of a gravel road before continuing its plunge down and to the right. You can't lose your way from here. Just follow the path until it comes to a fairly abrupt end at the cliff face you first encountered just above the gravel road. Retrace your way down the log steps for the last few minutes.

Constantia Nek

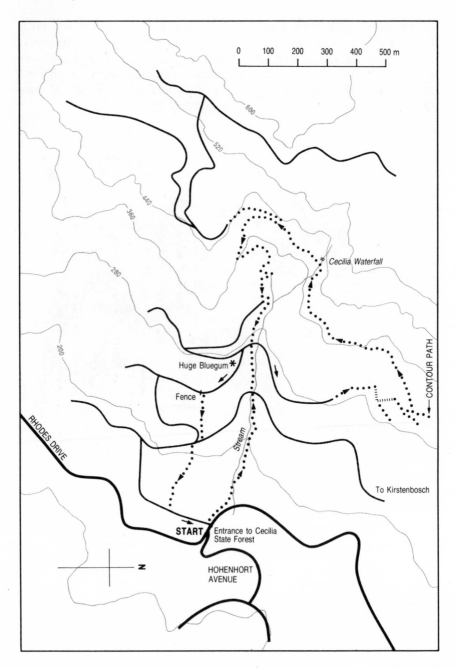

CECILIA WATERFALL   *16*

Time: *2 hours*
Grade: *2A*
Water: *Available*

This is a great walk if your time is limited and you want to work up a good sweat. The waterfall is well worth the sweat, for it is surely one of the loveliest in the Cape Peninsula. Covered in thick green moss, it is probably at its best when reduced to a trickle in mid-summer.

Leave your car at the entrance to the Cecilia State Forest (named after Cecil John Rhodes) opposite Hohenhort Drive on the road between Kirstenbosch and Constantia Nek. Hop over the wooden fence where it ends at the main road and follow the wire fence in the direction of Cape Town until you cross a stream about 100 m further on. A faint path goes up the side of the stream, mostly on its right bank (going up). Five minutes up the stream you pass a crude wooden footbridge. Do not cross over it, rather continue up the right bank for another 5 minutes until the clear path takes you over a forestry road. Cross over to the left bank and continue up for yet another 5 minutes until you come to a point where three forestry roads and some more log steps meet. There is a huge bluegum at the confluence of all four. Take the narrow road sharp right: this is the Contour Path which starts at Constantia Nek and ends at Kloof Nek (see Chapters 20, 21 and 22). You'll come back to this meeting of the ways at the end of your circular route.

Soon the road peters out into a narrow path. Notice that the pine trees are of a particular type (*Pinus radiata*). They are commercially viable because all the knots appear at regular intervals where the branches radiate out from one point on the trunk. Also the main trunk is straight, as opposed to the pine commonly grown in gardens and particularly noticeable on Rondebosch Common, *Pinus pinaster*, which sends out branches in all directions as it pleases. Try making straight poles out of that. Further on you'll reach some huge bluegums; they may be aliens, but they are majestic.

The path makes a U-bend around a little ravine and immediately climbs nine log steps. Fifteen paces beyond the top step turn off the path and climb up another more substantial set of steps to the left. On emerging from the Kirstenbosch edge of the bluegums, a sign directs you to the left (Cecilia Ravine). Ten metres past the sign a path leaves the Contour Path sharply up to the left. Take this log staircase, stopping every now and again to admire the view. Below lies the Kirstenbosch Dam, used to irrigate the world-famous Botanical Gardens. This is one of the more pleasant 'up' climbs I can think of: hard work, but rewarding. In no time at all, thanks to well-placed and carefully maintained steps, you are high up, and lovely views begin to unfold. Notice the indigenous Cape Cypress on either side of you, which is often mistaken for Hakea, an alien invader.

Five or six minutes after leaving the Contour Path up the log staircase, you will reach your first high point. Thereafter it descends through a tight ravine overgrown with indigenous vegetation and ascends the other side for more splendid views, with a bird's eye view over the canopy of Cecilia Forest. Also notice Wynberg Hill beyond.

About a quarter of an hour after leaving the Contour Path, you will reach the second high point. This is a good spot to rest and admire the view for a short while. Not too long though, for just around the corner is the reward for all your effort. You will be looking into two ravines merging into one. The zigzag path on the far side is on the slope of Spilhaus Ravine (your down route), and the nearer, dense indigenous forest grows in Cecilia Ravine. The waterfall is reached some 7 minutes after leaving your rest place at the second high point.

It is a lovely spot, full of peace and tranquillity. About 18 m high and covered in moss, the waterfall almost always has water. There is a faint path up the right-hand side of the waterfall, but don't be tempted to climb up this path, as you'll only contribute to soil erosion and it doesn't go anywhere. Any attempt to get to the top of the waterfall is fraught with danger, so remain at peace and admire it from below.

After you have refreshed your body and soul, climb up and out of Cecilia Ravine and see your zigzag route down. About 6 minutes after leaving the waterfall, the path reaches its highest point. At this spot log steps go up and off to the right. This is not your route, but it does mark the top of your climb. These steps join the Bridle Path back to Constantia Nek (see the rock cutting above and ahead of you). Your way, thankfully, is now all down, and a gentle down at that.

About 15 minutes of descent will bring you to some concrete settling tanks which must once have been used for water purification. Don't follow the jeep track you now see, but rather step over the noisy plastic water pipe to the left and follow the path down to the river. Although this is known as the Old Picnic Site, a regular climbing friend of mine

Cecilia Waterfall

prefers to call it 'Bacon-and-Eggs Corner', because we have detected that gorgeous aroma from 100 m up! Five minutes down the river from 'Bacon-and-Eggs Corner' brings you back to the four-way intersection with its huge bluegum you passed earlier.

From here you can either return the way you came up, following the river, or for variety take a different but equally rewarding route back to the car. If you choose the latter, follow the road down in the direction of the foresters' cottages, around and to the left of the bluegum. Close on 300 m down, you will see a fence and the foresters' accommodation. Leave the road and go down the side of the fence until you reach another gravel road, then turn right. Just after the hairpin bend the path again leaves the road and wanders down through pine forest straight back to your car.

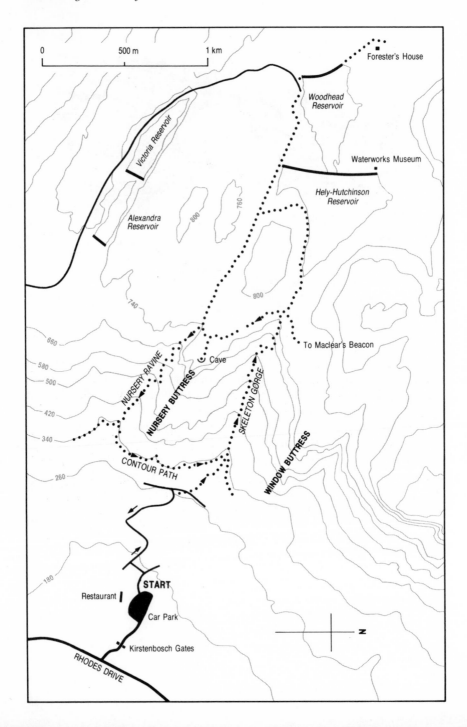

SKELETON GORGE AND NURSERY RAVINE

17

Time: $3\frac{1}{2}$ *hours*
Grade: *3B*
Water: *Available*

Skeleton Gorge is probably one of the most popular routes up Table Mountain. The other two routes that carry heavy traffic, namely Kasteelspoort above Camps Bay and Platteklip Gorge above the City Bowl, are not nearly as pleasant, as they are much more exposed to the sun and the more inclement weather.

Skeleton Gorge on the other hand is an excellent climb on a hot summer's day as it is almost entirely in the shade at all times. Furthermore this is not just any old shade, but the kind provided by majestic Milkwood, Red Alder, Wild Peach, Yellowwood, Assegaaibos and other indigenous trees.

Drive through the main entrance gates to Kirstenbosch Botanical Gardens (a modest charge is levied, so have your cash ready). The road leads to a large parking area where you leave your car. At the far end of the parking area is the Botanical Society's Bookshop, and lower down the Tea Garden and Restaurant. Your starting point is the top left-hand corner of the parking area. Facing the mountain, turn left into a gravel walkway clearly marked 'Skeleton Gorge, Smuts' Track and Contour Path'. Another three such signs will lead you past a rectangular concrete reservoir after about 10 minutes. Notice the interesting float control on top of it, indicating the level of the water. About 3 minutes beyond the reservoir you'll come to another sign saying 'Dogs should be kept on a leash at all times'. At this point leave the gravel road and go up the log path. You will cross over the road again, as it doubles back on itself.

Another sign leads you on to the Contour Path, Skeleton Gorge and the Back Table. The log staircase in front of you is neatly spaced. The sounds of running water and the chirping of insects, a gentle breeze and luxurious shade, all combine to make this a most pleasant setting. No wonder it was General Jan Smuts' favourite part of Mother Mountain. There's no mistaking the Contour Path when you reach it. Where you cross over it on your upward stroll, there is a metal plaque on a rock where the great statesman used to take a breather. You might like to do the same. This is the point back to which you'll be coming after descending Nursery Ravine.

Continue your upward climb along what must be the best maintained path on all of Table Mountain. It keeps to the left side of the gorge for about half the way up, then leads you to a 2-metre ladder which makes it much easier to scramble up the rock face at this point. It then continues up the river bed in a deep, narrow section of the gorge to a gabion (a loose stone wall held together with wire mesh) damming up the river above: the gabion probably helps to make this section passable in winter. At the gabion turn right and cross the river onto a zigzag path which winds its way up through gorgeous ferns, their rich greenness shimmering in the filtered sunlight. Ignore a path going off to the right – this leads to a small overhang cave.

Near the top of the narrow zigzag path are some huge Red Alders (Rooiels or Butterspoon Trees). The path crosses over the gorge again and from here you can look down on your car way below. Just beyond a spot where you cross over back onto the left bank there is a spot against the dripping rock face where Red Disa (*Disa uniflora*, also justifiably named The Pride of Table Mountain) grow. Keep a sharp eye open for them in January and February. I recently saw no less than forty here in an area of no more than three square metres.

On reaching the top you'll be confronted by a huge boulder. Some call it 'Breakfast Rock', but I never seem to get there early enough. The path continues for a few metres to the right and beyond Breakfast Rock to a metal signpost with three direction pointers on it. Skeleton Gorge points the way you've just come, Maclear's Beacon indicates the direction of the path to the right and Kasteelspoort is straight ahead. Oddly enough you need to turn left at this point in the only direction that isn't indicated! The path picks its way faintly up the slope and in a few short minutes you'll be at the top. Look back at the sheer drop of Hiddingh Buttress above Newlands, and nearer at hand at the startlingly bright red Crassula growing out of seemingly inhospitable cracks in the rock from January to March.

Once over the top you start to descend into Nursery Ravine, but after about only 50 m look out for a path going off sharply to the left. This is an extremely worthwhile 3-minute detour to a substantial cave with superb views and excellent shelter from the sun or rain.

Retrace your steps to the main path, which will soon bring you to the top of the steep Nursery Ravine. From here down to the Contour Path

it is a steep, bone-jarring descent, made worthwhile by some of the best stands in the Peninsula of King Protea (*P. cynaroides*), our national flower, from February to April. Such steep descents need to be done either slowly, one step at a time, or on the trot. I prefer the latter, which gets me down to the Contour Path in a mere 20 minutes.

Once you reach the Contour Path and have given yourself enough time for the Shaking Legs Syndrome to disappear, turn left to get back to Kirstenbosch. It's mostly on the level and looks down on the lovely gardens and rolling lawns interspersed with footpaths and patches of indigenous bush. Ten minutes' walking along the Contour Path will bring you to the metal plaque you saw earlier, and a right-hand turn takes you down and back to your car. A welcome cooldrink or tea at the restaurant might not be out of place.

Doing this walk the other way round is not recommended. Nursery Ravine is too steep for comfort on the way up, and doesn't provide nearly as much shade.

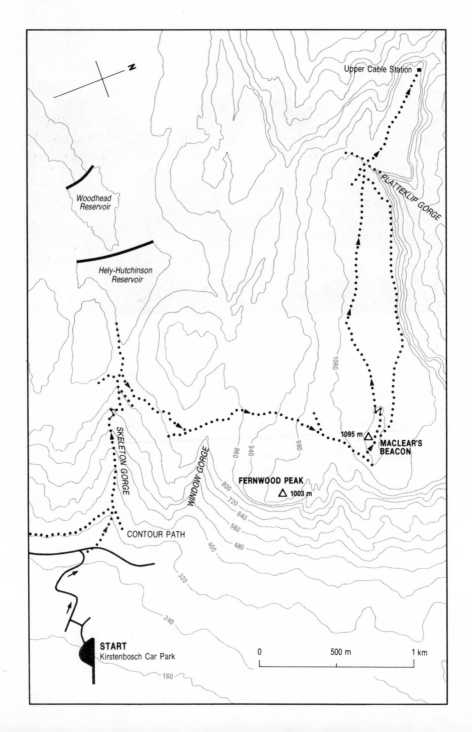

SMUTS' TRACK   *18*

Time: $4\frac{1}{2}$ *hours (one way)*
Grade: *4B*
Water: *Available*

This classic walk is surprisingly strenuous considering it was named after a man who regularly walked this route even when well into his seventies. It starts from Kirstenbosch, ascends Skeleton Gorge and ends at Maclear's Beacon, the highest point on Table Mountain, at the opposite end of the table top to the Upper Cable Station. For the purpose of this walk, we will carry on to the Upper Cable Station so as to take the easy way down in the cable car. This means that you need to have a car at each end. Check first that the cable car is operating, and take enough money with you for the fare, otherwise you'll have to get down via Platteklip Gorge, for which you will need to add another hour.

Jan Christiaan Smuts (1870-1950) left an indelible mark on South African history and made no small contribution to international events of this century. At Yalta he sat shoulder to shoulder with Stalin, Eisenhower and Churchill, and he was one of the architects of the United Nations. He walked this route for 50 years, more times than you and I have had Sunday dinners. Think of this remarkable man as you climb. I have a strange idea I may have met him, but more of that later on.

Having left another car at the Lower Cable Station, park your car in the parking area of Kirstenbosch Botanical Gardens. (There is a small charge to enter the gardens.) Start from the top left-hand corner of the parking area, where you will find a signpost showing you the way to Smuts' Track and Skeleton Gorge. Wherever there is a junction in the gravel road that follows, you will find another signpost pointing you in the right direction to Smuts' Track and Skeleton Gorge. After 15 to 20 minutes of upward stroll along the gravel road, you will reach a point where log steps lead straight up, with the usual helpful signpost. Leave the road at this point and start the strenuous but tranquil walk up Skeleton Gorge. Most of the way up, the path is well maintained and is characterised by comfortably positioned log steps.

Keep an eye open for nameplates on the indigenous trees. These carry various bits of information regarding the trees. First the family to which it belongs, then the Latin name, followed by its Afrikaans and English common names and finally the tree number. This reference can be looked up in any national tree index, thus making all the previous information unnecessary!

About 100 m after leaving the gravel road you might notice one nameplate in particular which rather tickled me. There's nothing unusual about the Common Turkey-Berry, except its Afrikaans name. *Gewone bokdrol* describes the fallen berries perfectly.

Most times the river flowing down Skeleton Gorge is a babbling brook but occasionally, after heavy rain, it gives out a thunderous roar. At times like this, this walk should rather be left for fair weather, as a short section near the top of Skeleton Gorge runs up the river bed.

Ten minutes after leaving the gravel road you will reach the Contour Path (Chapters 20 and 21). At this point a bronze plaque set into a rock announces 'Smuts' Track', and you know you are on the right path. After a brief rest continue the upward slog through this magnificent indigenous forest. Half an hour later you will reach a couple of ladders that help you over a tricky part. Shortly beyond the ladders the route is forced into the river bed by the surrounding cliffs. You then reach a gabion (a wall of loose stones held together by wire mesh).

At this point the path zigzags up the right-hand slope, passes below a cave and finally emerges from the forest to reveal a superb view of the Cape Flats. The trees now below you are Rooiels (Red Alder). These huge and ancient specimens are quite the finest examples of these indigenous trees I have seen. Another name for Rooiels is Butterspoon Tree, named after the shape of the apical leaf at each growing tip.

About $1\frac{1}{2}$ hours after your start you should reach the top of Skeleton Gorge. Here you will find a metal signpost, where you will no doubt wish to rest. A few metres further on are the upper reaches of the Hely Hutchinson Reservoir. That is not your way, however, and you'll get a much better view of it from on high. Turn right and follow the sign to Maclear's Beacon. The path is well defined, and as long as you keep heading in a northerly direction you can't go wrong. From the top of Skeleton Gorge the path climbs steeply for 6 or 7 minutes before levelling out for a while. Notice Junction Peak on your left, and the imposing hulk of Fernwood Peak dead ahead.

Twenty minutes after leaving Skeleton Gorge you reach the top of Window Gorge, an area where Red and Mauve Disas abound in summer. After crossing the Window Gorge stream the path ascends the slopes of Fernwood Peak. Some way up, notice the aqueduct over to the left. Follow the cairns on the upward scramble and 10 – 15 minutes later you will see ahead of you a pointed pinnacle on the left and a weirdly shaped overhanging block on the right. The path finds its way between these two landmarks.

Immediately beyond the overhanging block the path veers sharp right for a few metres, and then straightens out again to reveal another signpost. A sharp left turn would take you to Kasteelspoort, but your way is straight on, despite the fact that the signpost is a bit askance: the way is clear enough. About 8 minutes beyond the signpost you come to some simple rock scrambles. Just before these, look out for a rocky cairn almost hidden in the bush on the right which marks a faint path off to the right through waist-high fynbos. It leads to Carrell's Ledge, a sensational traverse along a narrow ledge which eventually brings you to the same spot you are headed anyway. This is the crazy alternative, however, and only for those who have absolutely no fear of heights and are full of the-devil-may-care. Ropes are not necessary.

Normal people should continue up the rock scramble at the top of which there is a fork. Take the more obvious left-hand alternative, and you're almost there. Two minutes later there is another signpost, and 50 m further on the stone pyramid of Maclear's Beacon itself. Read all about it on the bronze plaque on the beacon. Near the beacon, 15 m to the north of the signpost, is the Mountain Club War Memorial, which was dedicated on 25 February 1923 by General (later Field Marshal) J.C. Smuts.

When I did this particular walk for the purposes of writing this account, I was pressed for time due to publishers' deadlines, and was obliged to do it in the foulest of weather, by myself, which was foolish on at least two counts, but could not be avoided. It was absolutely pouring with rain, the wind was howling and visibility was down to about 20 m. Suddenly, out of the mist, came an old man dressed in rain gear, so that I could only see his eyes and nose and grey beard through his anorak. I called out to him and said, 'I thought I was the only one crazy enough to be on the mountain today'. He stopped and looked at me and said, 'Surprisingly mild, actually,' and then he turned and disappeared into the mist. As I write, I wonder about that old man. Was he real, or was I affected by the extreme weather conditions, or could it be that he was ...? No, surely not!

From Maclear's Beacon follow the yellow-and-white footprints painted on the rocks in reverse (in other words, walk against the direction of the footprints). This will bring you, within about half an hour, to the head of Platteklip Gorge (the 'nick' in the middle of the otherwise flat table top). On the way notice the superb view of the Table Mountain reservoirs, the two main ones built nearly a century ago. At that time they supplied all of Cape Town's needs, but today the combined capacity of all five reservoirs when full to the brim would provide Cape Town with water for only about five days.

The path descends into the 'nick' of Platteklip Gorge and then ascends again onto the Western Table. The Upper Cable Station and Restaurant are about ten minutes' walk from the top of Platteklip Gorge.

Maclear's Beacon

DEVIL'S PEAK

19

Time: *6 hours*
Grade: *4D (This route is for experienced mountaineers only)*
Water: *Available on lower slopes*

There are easier ways up Devil's Peak than Mowbray Ridge, the Knife Edge Path and the direct route for the final assault, but none so exciting and rewarding – provided you have a head for heights. If you just want to get there to say you've been to the top, then take the zigzag path up the Saddle from Tafelberg Road, then straight up the firebreak. But that seems far too much like jogging to me, a sort of monotonously self-inflicted punishment in the name of exercise.

The route I'm suggesting takes in a bit of everything: gentle indigenous forest walks, a view of two oceans, and paths that in places seem to be on the very edge of the world. Nowhere are ropes required; merely keep to the path. However, as indicated by the grading of this walk, do not attempt this one if you have a fear of heights or are unfit.

Start at Rhodes Memorial. Set off from the top right-hand corner of the parking area, where there are log steps ascending steeply towards the King's Blockhouse on the horizon above. This is your first objective, and it will take you 35 to 40 minutes to reach it. On your way up, there seem to be two Devil's Peaks. The one on the right is Minor Peak, although from this particular angle it appears to be a twin because it is closer to you.

Shortly before reaching the King's Blockhouse you come to a T-junction. Turn left, and a minute later you reach the Contour Path straddled by a turnstile and ladder. Pass through the turnstile (for some strange reason children always seem to prefer the more difficult route up the ladder) and veer left up the gravel road for about 100 m. Then climb up some steep log steps which will bring you right under the barrels of a couple of cannons guarding the King's Blockhouse, built by the British during their first occupation of the Cape between 1795 and 1803.

Now climb to the circular concrete reservoir behind the King's Blockhouse, where there is almost always water. This is the start of the climb up Mowbray Ridge. Going off to the right is the continuation of the Contour Path from Constantia Nek to Kloof Nek, but your way is straight up, behind the reservoir. Soon you will be confronted by rock

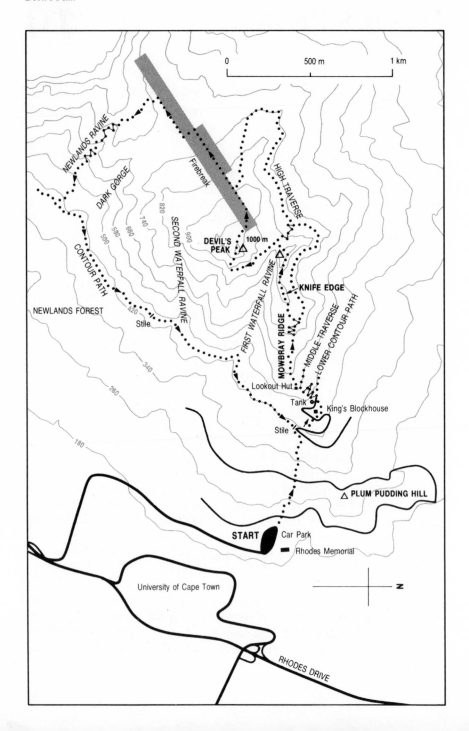

scrambles (steep, but not difficult) and views that alternate between Table Bay and False Bay.

Your next objective is the lookout hut, which you might have noticed earlier, perched on the cliff above. About 20 minutes after leaving the King's Blockhouse and just below the hut, you should see a faint path to the right, marked by a small cairn. This is the so-called Middle Traverse or 580-m Traverse. It does a half-circle around Devil's Peak to the saddle on the other side. Do not take it, but rather continue up the rocky face to the lookout hut above. The hut is a good spot for a rest, with spectacular views on both sides of the ridge.

When starting off from the lookout hut after your rest, take note of the time, for it is important that you do not miss the next turning some 15 minutes further up. From the hut, the path follows the ridge up to a point where it begins to zigzag sharply. On the fifth bend another less well-defined path continues straight up. This is the Knife Edge path. The main path which continues to the right and leaves the ridge is the High Traverse or 700-m Traverse. It circles Minor Peak and takes you to a point 100 m below the nek between Minor Peak and Devil's Peak (see map) and eventually continues around Oppelskop Ridge and up Devil's Peak. However, rather continue up the ridge and opt for the less obvious path straight up. This is the breathtaking Knife Edge Path,

which is not nearly as ominous as its name suggests, but nevertheless is probably the highlight of the walk.

This path takes you along the spine of Minor Peak with precipitous drops on either side, particularly on the left looking down into First Waterfall Ravine. Notice how the rock face below the summit of Devil's Peak has been forced into dramatic contortions by what must have been immense pressures on the sedimentary rock millions of years ago.

Near the summit of Minor Peak some simple rock scrambling takes you between two huge boulders which form a gateway at the top right. A brief scramble down the other side takes you to the nek between Devil's Peak and Minor Peak and the top of First Waterfall Ravine. **Do not** attempt to go around Minor Peak to the left. From here the direct route to the summit is on a path which climbs straight up and slightly to the left to get to the rock face above. The path is steep, but is marked by various cairns along the route. Once at the rock face (about 20 minutes after leaving the nek below Minor Peak), the path veers sharply to the left. Keep close to the rock face for about 150 m along a terrace, until the path peters out. A rocky cairn now indicates a change of direction straight up for about 10 m to get you onto the topmost terrace. This narrow terrace and precipitous path works its way around the corner, onto the east face for about 100 m. Again you run out of terrace. Look for the obvious way up a 50-m rock scramble to the summit. It should take you about $3\frac{1}{2}$ hours to reach the summit from the start.

Your route down is to the Saddle via the firebreak, and from there down Newlands Ravine and along the Contour Path back to Rhodes Memorial. Allow a fraction under 2 hours for the return. On leaving the summit, make for the third trig beacon (the westernmost of the three at or near the top of Devil's Peak). At this beacon the path forks: take the left-hand fork, which will lead you down the firebreak to the Saddle between Table Mountain and Devil's Peak. Twenty minutes later you should reach the Saddle, but be careful of your footing, for the scree is slippery, particularly in wet weather. Leading down from the saddle on the Newlands side are three ravines: Dark Gorge, Newlands Ravine and Els Ravine. The first and last require ropes and are particularly dangerous to anyone not familiar with mountaineering techniques. They should therefore be avoided by the casual hiker. Don't be fooled into thinking that the middle ravine is the one going down from the middle of the Saddle. That is in fact Dark Gorge, which is as ominous as its name implies. The start of Newlands Ravine is on the far side of the Saddle and you need to climb part of the way up the far side of the Saddle before turning left. There should be signposts guiding you to the top of Newlands Ravine, assuming mindless vandals haven't broken them.

The descent down Newlands Ravine to the Contour Path should take about 30 to 40 minutes. It is steep but well defined, with stone steps most of the way. You will know you are near the end of the bone-jarring descent when you get to the skeleton of a huge dead tree some 6 or 7 minutes from the relative peace and tranquillity of the Contour Path.

At the Contour Path, turn left and head for home. It will take about another half an hour to get to the turnstile just below the King's Blockhouse, but the walk is a quiet, gentle one through dense forest, starkly contrasting with what you have been through. Once back at the King's Blockhouse turnstile, retrace your steps to Rhodes Memorial and perhaps enjoy a refresher at the tearoom there, if it's not too full of daytrippers with far less energy than yourself!

King's Blockhouse

Contour Path: Constantia Nek to Kirstenbosch

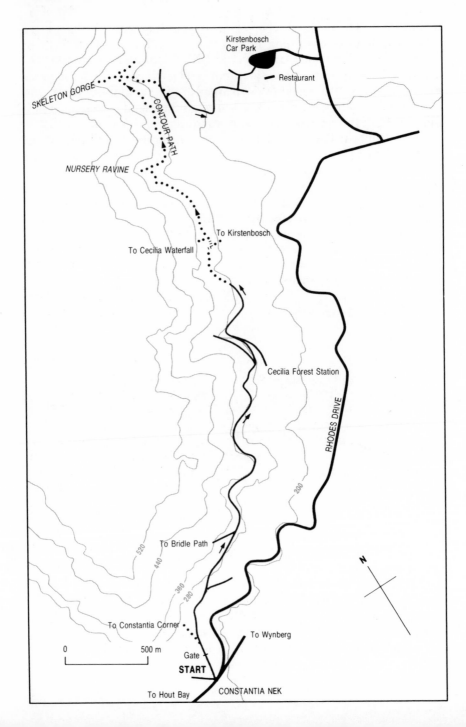

CONTOUR PATH: CONSTANTIA NEK TO KIRSTENBOSCH

20

Time: $1\frac{3}{4}$ *hours one way*
Grade: *1A*
Water: *Available*

This is a leisurely stroll through forest and fynbos and is suitable for the whole family. If you're wise you'll have a friend's car waiting for you at Kirstenbosch, and remember that the restaurant there serves an excellent breakfast or brunch. This is also a gentle walk that can be done at any time of the day or year, as it is mostly in shade so a hot summer's morning or sunny winter's afternoon can be equally pleasant. In fact you could even do it dressed in your Sunday best. Not that this form of attire is recommended, but I have seen numerous overly well-dressed people on this walk, so it must be all right.

Start at Constantia Nek. A narrow tarred road leaves the Wynberg side of the picnic area and travels up for about 200 m before coming to a closed gate. A few metres beyond the gate log steps ascend to the left, but ignore them and continue along the gravel road for about 4 minutes until you come to a fork in the road. Take the left fork up. After a further 8 minutes or so, the road doubles back on itself opposite a steel road barrier. Don't double back, but rather carry on. (To turn sharp left would take you to the dams and the Back Table along the so-called Bridle Path – actually a road.) Carrying on along the straight, you'll soon come out into the open, with splendid views of the Cape Flats and False Bay. A little koppie on the right offers a grandstand view. At this point the road does a sharp 90-degree left turn and about 10 minutes later the black-tiled roofs of the Cecilia Forest Officer's home come into view, as does a giant bluegum at a fork in the road. It's hardly necessary to say keep right at the fork, as the left alternative is obviously less used. Keep right then, and soon you'll come to a major intersection. At this intersection three roads and a set of log steps all come together. One road is behind you, one doubles back 180 degrees to the right to the foresters' cottages, and one goes 90 degrees to the right. The steps on the left come down from Cecilia Waterfall (see Chapter 16). The way you need to go is the road going 90 degrees to the right.

Soon the road narrows to a path and shortly after it does a little U-bend around a small ravine, and then climbs nine log steps. Some fifteen paces on turn sharp left up some more steep log steps. At this point you seem to be leaving the Contour Path, but you're not. You're just getting back up to the right level. This is the point where most people go wrong, so read carefully!

Having climbed up the steep log steps, you'll soon come to a notice at a fork in the path. Right and down will take you to the southern outskirts of Kirstenbosch Gardens. You need to keep left to continue on the Contour Path, but beware. Having taken the left fork up, it almost immediately doubles back on itself. **Do not** double back, but rather carry on along the less obvious straight path. If you take the more obvious route up, you will eventually reach Cecilia Waterfall (see Chapter 16). Remember that you are on a contour path which, as the name implies, means you should remain more or less on the same level.

Now you are out of the forest and into the fynbos. A few minutes further on you'll meet a path coming up from Kirstenbosch. Ignore it and continue a few more metres to the bottom of Nursery Ravine (a sign set into a rock tells you that you have arrived there). Keep going along the Contour Path, now delightfully wrapped in indigenous forest. Ten minutes later you will reach the point where the Contour Path crosses Skeleton Gorge, and here another plaque announces 'Smuts' Track'. At this point turn down the well-marked path which will lead you to the Kirstenbosch restaurant some 15 minutes later. Enjoy your late breakfast of bacon and eggs, not to mention champagne and orange juice.

CONTOUR PATH: KIRSTENBOSCH TO RHODES MEMORIAL

21

Time: *3 hours (one way)*
Grade: *2A*
Water: *Available*

Like the first part of the Contour Path from Constantia Nek to Kirsten-bosch, this section is also almost entirely in shade. It's a little more strenuous, though, as part of it belies its description of 'contour' path and zigzags up to a point about 150 m higher up the slopes of Fernwood Buttress before plummeting back down again.

The indigenous forest through which it meanders is quite remarkable for its diversity. The authorities have clearly labelled the main trees of the forest, and familiar names such as Yellowwood, Assegaai, Cape Saffron, Wild Almond, Ironwood and Rooiels are much in evidence. Start the walk at the car park next to the Kirstenbosch restaurant. (There is a small charge to take your car into the Botanical Gardens.) At the top left-hand corner of the parking area there is a sign indicating the way to Skeleton Gorge, Smuts' Track and the Contour Path. Follow the sign and subsequent ones along this gravel road and some 15 minutes later you reach some log steps leaving the gravel road. (This point is marked by a sign informing you that dogs should be on a leash.) Ten minutes up these well-built log steps brings you to the Contour Path.

At this point you'll want a rest. Sit on the same rock regularly used for a breather by former world statesman Field Marshal Jan Christiaan Smuts. A bronze plaque announces 'Smuts' Track' and it refers to the beginning of a long but fascinating trek to the highest point on Table Mountain which was followed regularly by the 'Oubaas' (see Chapter 18). Having taken in the peace and tranquillity of this resting place, so enjoyed by Smuts, take solace in the fact that your upward slog is temporarily over.

Follow the broad Contour Path in a northerly direction towards Cape Town. Fifty metres on, cross a stream (which can be a raging torrent after heavy rain). This is the stream which tumbles down Skeleton

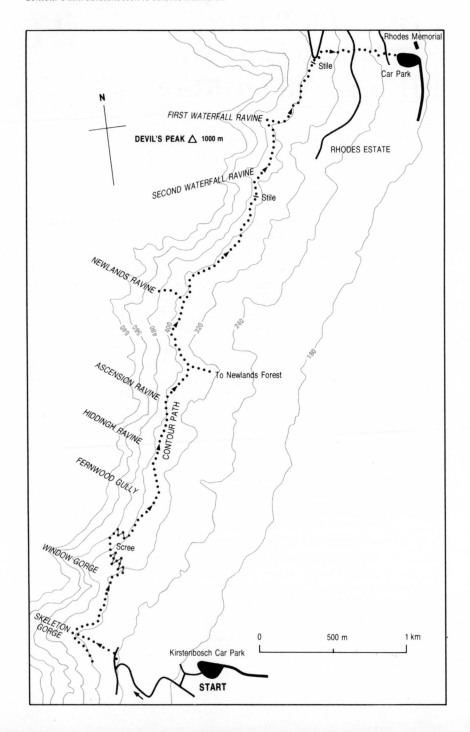

Gorge, and here it becomes a most spectacular waterfall when the river is flowing strongly.

About 10 minutes further on you find yourself crossing another river course in the next ravine (Window Gorge). Along the way you might have noticed, amongst the indigenous trees of the forest, some oak trees which have been ringbarked: enough to make Simon van der Stel turn over in his grave several times, but they **are** intruders, after all.

Five minutes beyond Window Gorge you reach a most important fork in the path; important because most people who don't know better tend to turn right and find themselves back in Kirstenbosch. Your way is left and up, despite the fact that the so-called 'Contour Path' no longer follows the contour. In fact, the path now follows a zigzag route up the lower slopes of Fernwood Buttress for about 20 minutes, finally reaching fallen scree at its highest point. This is perhaps a good point at which to take a breather and enjoy some refreshments.

Surprisingly the way seems quite clear across the scree, after which it drops fairly steeply for 5 minutes until you come to a huge boulder on the right (all of 4 m high and 8 m long). Now you are back on the level again, but the path becomes fairly rocky and uneven for about 10 minutes until it takes you into Fernwood Gully, followed in quick succession by Wormhole Ravine and Hiddingh Ravine. Soon afterwards you will find the Newlands Forest path joining you from the right and 10 minutes later the Newlands Ravine path comes down steeply from the left. (This is your way down from Devil's Peak in Chapter 19.) Keep going on past two deep, dry ravines until you reach a stile some 15 minutes beyond the Newlands Ravine path.

You are now on the slopes of Devil's Peak. Go through the stile and ladder which separates Newlands Forest from Groote Schuur Estate – Cecil John Rhodes' gift to South Africa – which includes the University of Cape Town. Your walk through Groote Schuur Estate will take another 15 to 20 minutes, past Second Waterfall and First Waterfall ravines, until eventually you reach another stile and ladder.

In between the stiles marking the boundaries of the estate are cliffs cloaked in forest, including some truly majestic bluegums. Notice, however, that nothing else grows underneath them, which is why these Australian invaders are regarded as unwelcome guests. Their insatiable thirst robs the ground of moisture which would otherwise be available to others.

At the second stile, turn down to the right. Notice the King's Block-house up to the left. After a recent fire, I was alarmed to see black wattle (another Australian invader) springing up everywhere. Cecil John Rhodes might have had tremendous entrepreneurial and political talent, but of environmental foresight he had none!

Now comes the only unpleasant part of this walk, down log steps which seem to be so spaced as to jar every bone in your body. It lasts only for 10 to 15 minutes before you reach the car you wisely have waiting for you at Rhodes Memorial.

Rhodes died in 1902 and 10 years later, on his birthday, 5th July 1912, this memorial was erected on one of his favourite viewpoints. It was designed by Sir Herbert Baker and funded by public contributions. But Rhodes' real memorial is perhaps the University of Cape Town, for he donated the land on which it stands today. Appropriately, any letters posted at UCT post office are franked 'Rhodes' Gift'.

Another serious proposal after his death, was to place a 50-storey high 'Colossus of Rhodes', perched on top of Lion's Head. Thank heavens we finished up with this lesser edifice on the slopes of Devil's Peak.

Rhodes Memorial

CONTOUR PATH: RHODES MEMORIAL TO KLOOF NEK

22

Time: $3\frac{1}{2}$ *hours one way. Add half an hour to explore Woodstock Cave.*
Grade: *2C*
Water: *Available*

This is a walk with a substantial cave to explore and a breathtaking view of Table Mountain which is thrust upon you all of a sudden. The only reason it's graded 'C' is because of one short stretch above the end of Tafelberg Road where the path is moderately exposed. Otherwise it's an 'A' all the way. You will need two cars if you don't wish to walk back.

Leave your first car 800 m up the road from Kloof Nek towards the Lower Cable Station. There is suitable off-road parking just below the second hairpin bend. From here to Rhodes Memorial is 12 km by road, but don't worry as you will only be walking about 8 km back. When leaving your car at the starting point, don't do as my wife did to us, and finish up with the wrong keys for the right cars!

Having parked your car in the Rhodes Memorial parking area, set off up the log steps at the top right-hand corner. Your immediate aim is the King's Blockhouse on the horizon above. It's going to take you about 40 minutes to get there, so put your head down and set to it.

From this angle Devil's Peak seems to have a twin. The 'twin' on the right is Minor Peak. When seen from afar, however, it is clear that it is very much a younger demon. The log steps are well spaced for going up one step at a time, but bone-jarring coming down. At the top of the steps you are confronted by a T-junction. Turn left, and in a minute or so you'll reach the Contour Path. Go through the turnstile on your right and up the gravel road ascending half left. About 100 m up, leave the road for a shortcut to the King's Blockhouse directly above.

On arrival at the King's Blockhouse you deserve a rest. This place is officially known on survey maps as the King's Battery and was built by the British during their first occupation of the Cape between 1795 and 1803. Its guns were never fired in anger, but at one time it was used to accommodate convict labour during afforestation of Devil's Peak in the

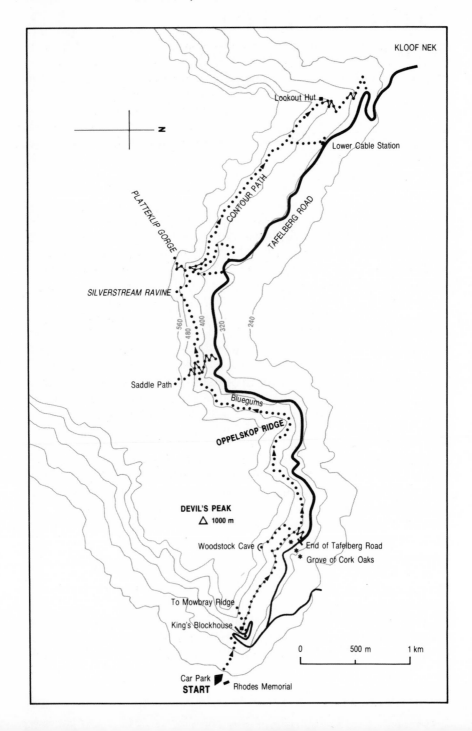

latter part of the 19th century. It is an excellent viewpoint, and one cannot help admiring the forester who had a substantial house up here about a hundred years ago. Two oceans can be seen clearly, and also pick out the Liesbeek River, Groote Schuur Hospital, Newlands Rugby and Cricket Grounds and the University of Cape Town

Find your way to behind the King's Blockhouse where you will see a small concrete reservoir: there is always water here. The steps going up past the reservoir lead to Mowbray Ridge and up Devil's Peak. However, you don't wish to be quite so ambitious on this walk, so keep on the level to the right of and just below the reservoir. This is the so-called Lower Contour Path. It is in fact a continuation of the Contour Path from Constantia Nek but assumes the 'lower' designation here on Devil's Peak as there are also Middle and Upper Contour Paths.

Ten minutes after leaving the King's Blockhouse, the path curves into a ravine. Look up and see Woodstock Cave (occasionally known as Devil's Peak Cave). It is a substantial rock overhang 50 m wide by 15 m deep and 3-4 m high at the mouth. It is well worth a visit, but you need to go well past it, then zigzag up and double back to get there.

Below you on the right is a parking area marking the end of Tafelberg Road. The point at which to turn up to get to Woodstock Cave is just beyond a fascinating grove of trees which have bark like cork trees and acorns like oak trees, but leaves unlike either. These apparent mongrels are in fact Cork Oaks. About 100 m beyond the Cork Oak grove, a path comes up sharply from the road below and crosses the Contour Path to continue zigzagging up the slope. Take this deviation up and back to reach Woodstock Cave. Count the number of zigzags, and after the seventh one, just as you are confronted with a steep log step and rock scramble, leave the main path and head back towards the King's Blockhouse along a clear path which leads you straight to Woodstock Cave. From the Contour Path to the cave will take you about 13 minutes up and 7 minutes down.

Once at the cave, see Table Bay framed by its narrow mouth, and the ruins of the Queen's Blockhouse just below and to the right of the parking area. Having recharged your batteries and enjoyed the view from Woodstock Cave, get back to the Contour Path and continue in the direction of town. Soon Lion's Head thrusts itself into view, and in no time the scenery changes dramatically.

After part of Table Mountain comes into view behind Oppelskop Ridge, the path descends slowly, and after passing a turn-off back down to the tarred road, starts ascending again. Look down onto a beautiful pool alongside the road way below you. If you have a fear of heights, this is where you're going to feel it. Continue your steady upward climb. When you draw level with the first of the three 'pepper pots' (circular high-rise apartment blocks) to the right, a path climbs up steeply to the left. Do not take this path, but rather carry on along the level. This steep branch to the left connects with the Middle Contour Path.

A few minutes later, as you round Oppelskop Ridge, Table Mountain suddenly appears in all its magnificence and splendour. What an awe-inspiring surprise! The sheer visual impact of walking around what seems to be just another corner is quite breathtaking. The first time I rounded this corner, I walked back and did it twice again! Mother Mountain just seems to tower over you.

Ten minutes later you pass through a bluegum plantation and then start to change from walking on the slopes of Devil's Peak to Table Mountain itself. Soon the Saddle Path crosses the Contour Path. Notice the yawning gap of Platteklip Gorge: this is the 'nick' in the table top as seen from afar.

Ten to fifteen minutes after crossing the Saddle Path you arrive at Silverstream Ravine, just 5 minutes before you reach Platteklip Gorge. Silverstream is identifiable as a deep and pretty ravine, rich with indigenous trees except for four intrusive pines standing guard on the far side. There is almost always water here, and rock overhangs provide a welcome resting place. On reaching Platteklip Gorge, you will see two parallel paths traversing the buttress on the other side: take the higher one. The lower alternative takes you back to the tarred road well before you want to be there. The Contour Path is true to its name for the rest of the way, staying just below the cliff face.

A few hundred metres before you pass under the cableway, look up to the skyline ahead of you and see the 'venster' (window) after which Venster Buttress is named (see Chapter 2). The cableway goes up India Ravine, so named because it forms the outline of a map of India when seen from the city. As you pass under the cables, a path goes down to the right. This leads to the Lower Cable Station. As your car is further on, however, you should continue along the Contour Path to its very end. It's only another 5 minutes before you come to a stone lookout hut which marks the termination of the Contour Path which began at Constantia Nek, but you simply *must* peep around the corner to see Camps Bay from on high. Just below the lookout hut are some stone steps which will take you down to your waiting car in about 15 minutes. Hopefully you have the right keys.

FURTHER READING

Branch, Bill, *Field Guide to the Snakes and other Reptiles of Southern Africa*, Struik, Cape Town, 1988.

Broadley, D.G., *FitzSimons' Snakes of Southern Africa*, Delta Books, Johannesburg, 1983.

Burman, Jose, *Latest Walks in the Cape Peninsula*, Human & Rousseau, Cape Town, 1979.

Frandsen, Joy, *Birds of the South Western Cape*, Sable, Cape Town, 1982.

Green, Laurence, *Tavern of the Seas*, Howard Timmins, Cape Town, 1975.

Kench, John, *Know Table Mountain*, Chameleon Press, Bergvliet, Cape Town, 1988.

Kidd, Mary Maytham, *Cape Peninsula Wild Flower Guide*, Botanical Society of South Africa, Cape Town, 1983.

Marais, Johan, *Snakes versus Man*, Macmillan, Johannesburg, 1985.

Mountain Club of South Africa, *Table Mountain Guide*, MCSA, Cape Town, 1983.

Muir, John, *Know Your Cape*, Howard Timmins, Cape Town, 1975.

Pellant, Chris, *Earthscope*, Timmins, Cape Town, 1985.

Visser, John and Chapman, David, *Snakes and Snake Bite*, Purnell, Cape Town, 1978.

HIKING CLUBS

Mountain Club of South Africa, 97 Hatfield Street, Cape Town 8001.
Peninsula Ramblers, PO Box 982, Cape Town 8000.
South African Speleological Association, PO Box 4812, Cape Town 8000.
Trails Club of South Africa, PO Box 104, Diep River 7856.

INDEX